When
The Golden Eagle
Calls

When The Golden Eagle Calls

The story of a National Serviceman

Roger Northam

TO

SAe. R. HAMILTON

[signature]

MONTADA

First Published in Great Britain in 2006 by
Montada Publishing
64 Quarry Barton Hambrook
Bristol   BS16 1SG
Fax & Phone 01454-777108

First edition published 2006
This edition published 2007

The moral right of the author has been asserted

A CIP record for this book is available from the British Cataloguing in
Publication Data Office.

ISBN 978-0-9549011-1-0

Designed and typeset by Kakayen Associates.

Printed and bound by Antony Rowe Limited
Bumpers Farm Industrial Estate - Chippenham - Wiltshire - SN14 6LH

Other Titles By Author

66.n.o. Tales of a Village Cricketer

ISBN 0-9549011-0-X

CONTENTS

FOREWARD

I still don't quite know what to make of the two years I spent as a National Serviceman in the RAF. It did little to improve my creativity as a tyro weekly newspaper reporter whose career had reluctantly been put on hold. Nor in truth did it uplift me with any added sense of patriotism. But it did teach me how vigorously to polish my bed-space, how to darn my socks and sew my buttons; how to brush the floor and clean the billet stove with manic thoroughness on a Saturday morning if it preceded a 48-hour pass; how to salute in meaningless ritual bumptious young officers no older than I was; how to bellow my number on pay parade, and frantically to count the days to my next leave.

The cross section of human nature around me was part of the appeal. I missed Freddie Trueman by a week when I went to Padgate to collect my uniform. There were, however, a couple of professional footballers, a speedway rider from Norwich and a boxer from Bridgwater, who somehow fiddled time off to appear weekly in London on a Freddie Mills bill. He seldom won, getting a monumental black eye and £7 for his pains.

Square bashing at Hereford was a nightmare. I had completed my journalistic apprenticeship so I was two years older than my mates. That for some reason, more sadistic than rational, made me a sitting target for a trio of drill instructors, whose drunken and brutal habit was to return in the early hours and then order me out of bed to perform some absurd chore. The 'hilarious' alternative was to have me marching round the billet from a crouching position, with a heavy rifle on my boyish shoulders.

It seems that the idea was to break our spirits, so that they could more easily manipulate us. They didn't succeed. When next day we were engaged in bayonet practice, the blade went into the sandbags with screeching venom as we chose to imagine our drill instructors were the victims.

After Hereford, renowned in those days for the oafish contempt the corporals had for the recruits, many innocent and straight out of school, my National Service career was varied. For several months while waiting for posting, I was stationed in north London and seemed to spend my days helping to operate a homing device, located on the highest point of an allotment. The instruments were never explained to me – and I ceaselessly feared that I should be responsible for a mid-air crash.

Before any such fatality, I was whisked off on a Russian course for which I had volunteered on the mistaken belief that I might end up as the Moscow correspondent for The Times. We were told we might be given civilian status during the nine-month study period. It was nothing of the kind. The Combined Services camp was run by the Army, and we did an hour on the square every early morning, before going to the classrooms for the rest of the day.

The tutors, enlisted one can only imagine with difficulty, seemed to come from a hundred different countries, all with varying Russian accents and teaching ability. I lasted four months and then pleaded to be released.

I ended up at Thorney Island, near Portsmouth. It was a navigational station, full of greenhorn young Pilot Officers trying to direct their rattling Anson aircraft in roughly the right direction. It has to be said that the safety record wasn't too good. My modest duties involved plotting hazards for the pilots and distributing chocolate bars.

Maybe I should at least have exploited such a specialised RAF training by taking a village stores on my release, so that I could expertly recommend and hand out the best confectionery. But my enforced months in uniform weren't completely wasted. While stationed in London, I seemed to spend the whole of my 26 shillings a week taking the tube down to the West End. Servicemen were often able to get free tickets for under-subscribed London shows. I reckon I went to, and enjoyed, dozens of rotten plays and musicals. It was a rare privilege for a village lad like myself even to go. Very occasionally I dug into minimal capital and paid an eager visit to the nubile chorus girls at the Windmill.

For some wide-eyed teenagers, the institutionalised rigours of

National Service were timely and beneficial. They were shaped by the disciplines, improved as individuals by the excesses. Frankly it didn't do much for me. I dutifully carried out my instructions and resisted the system only in my head. I treasured the humour – graphically conveyed by the ebullient Roger Northam, a sporting mate and adversary from years ago – and the friendships. If I resented missing my burgeoning adventures as a junior reporter I kept it to myself. In its way my life in the RAF basically at the low rank from which I operated, was an evolving education.

Most of my time was as an AC2 – and you can't get any lower than that. In my final months, mostly as a result of my own resourcefulness as I searched for marginal improvement on payday, I miraculously found myself upgraded to AC1 and then, somehow, Leading Aircraftsman. I sewed the appropriate symbol on my sleeve with defiance rather than pride.

Sadly it has to be admitted I was an uncoordinated member of Her Majesty's finest. My uniform used to hang uneasily on me I regularly dropped and smashed my china mug in the NAAFI. One drill instructor back at Hereford, an obnoxious corporal I still dream fitfully about, would come within an inch of my face and bawl: "You're the sloppiest bastard in the unit – what are you?" And I was made to repeat the cringing self-condemnation.

On the day I left the RAF, my release papers recorded:
ABILITY – Adequate...APPEARANCE - Untidy.

MEAN SPIRITED TO THE END.

DAVID FOOT
2528404 – LAC

David Foot has written many books – mainly about sporting Icons of yesteryear - and is a highly respected journalist.

PREFACE

My friend Roger has recently published a successful and nostalgic book on events and personal experiences of local cricket in the Bristol area. This work has attracted much praise, and readers enjoyed the quality of his keen perception and humorous style.

Here he turns his attention to his two years National Service in the RAF. He considers this to have been an episode, which enriched his life in many ways, largely, I feel sure, because he had the wit to observe sympathetically the situations and characters he encountered.

I missed National Service, and having lived in penury whilst studying for accountancy examinations, was greatly relieved not to lose any more time before earning some money. There is a nagging doubt in my mind however, that I would have benefited by experiencing the hardships and disciplines of service life. Above all, I strongly suspect, I would have lost much of the reserve and desire for privacy, which are inhibiting characteristics to carry through life.

This book views National Service life with an observant eye, and will appeal both to those who have had similar experiences, and those who are not quite sure what they have missed.

Michael Wood

ACKNOWLEDGEMENTS

This book would not have been written but for the insistence of my son Kion, who never tired of hearing me 'tell the tale' (as 'old sweats' do).

I thank him therefore, for encouraging me to take up the pen and set my story down.

I would like to thank Geoff Husband for allowing me to use his wonderful painting of the Spitfire on the book cover, and to his son Geoff junior for his help in designing it.

Dave Shortman for his superb photographs and the other 'snappers' who contributed but whose names are now forgotten.

Thanks too to my Aden pals Rod Hamill and Bobbie Campbell for helping my memory along.

To Phill Zillwood for his wonderful interpretation of this book's cover.

Finally my grateful thanks to my ever-patient wife Parvin for letting an old man get on with reliving his happy youth.

HER MAJESTY CALLS

The majestic sight of steam engine numbered 6000 with its distinctive brass bell gleaming brightly at its front, and bearing the proud name of King George V, steamed into platform one of Temple Meads station toward, what must have looked a very forlorn fresh faced eighteen year old youth, standing alone clutching his battered little brown suitcase.

It was May 10th 1956 and that youth's life was about to change forever.

For I was off to do my duty.

I was on my way to Cardington in Bedfordshire to start my two years National Service in the RAF.

I was about to meet many new friends, and who knows, perhaps travel the world too.

It was all an exciting adventure.

But standing there, all alone, watching that hissing giant approach, I wasn't quite sure whether this strange tingling I was feeling was excitement, nerves, or just plain fear.

At least I was being carried to my fate by a King.

It had all started a couple of months earlier when that dreaded brown envelope with the letters O.H.M.S boldly showing on the flap, and addressed to R.K.Northam, plopped through the letter box at Brookside Cottage, Pye Corner, Hambrook, and mother handed it over with, I detected, a slight tremble of her loving hand.

"It's for you Rog. I think the call has come.

Her Majesty needs you."

Just seven days before, I had celebrated my eighteenth birthday and all was good in the world.

But mother was right. Here indeed was the dreaded call.

I was to report for a medical to an address in Clifton the following week.

In those days every young lad, on reaching the age of eighteen, had to serve his country by doing two years National Service. Most lads were enlisted in either the Army, the Navy or the Royal Air Force and were trained initially as fighting men good enough to defend their country. During the course of their two years they were also given some skill or other that many found more than useful when back in civvy street, from cooks to airframe fitters. The rigid discipline put many a wayward lad on the right path in life, and very few young lads came out of the services less than a better man.

Positively glowing with health, I presented myself to the medical board, and was examined in the minutest detail - hair, ears, and eyes. My eyesight, thank goodness, was excellent. I remember being able to read the printers name at the bottom of the card during the eye test:

"Iles Printers - Kingswood" I beamed broadly, only to be chastised firmly by the humourless medic.

"Stop fooling around and do as you are told lad," he growled.

But I did notice that later he went across to the list of letters - adjusted his spectacles - and grunted when he realised that I had been correct in my observation.

I was handed a book with nothing on its pages but a myriad of greyish dots. As the pages were slowly turned by the examiner, in the centre of each one these dots would form into numbers in various colours - some red - some blue - some green - and so on.

"Tell me exactly what you see," the medic said; and as page after page went by and I obediently read out the numbers that appeared, as if by magic, from the grey dots. Nine - eighteen - six - twenty five, and so on.

Suddenly (don't ask me why) I said, "A Spitfire."

It woke the old boy up and he irritably shut the book. After glowering at me for some moments he sat in silence making his copious notes on my records cards. 'Colour blind idiot', no doubt.

The medic was most concerned with my left ankle, which was badly deformed due to the effects of a stone thrown by one of the villagers when I was but four and a half years old. He called over two of his colleagues to study my old 'swinger', and they pulled and pushed it this way and that with great interest. I really had no proper ankle at all, as the joint had all fused together when the young bones were smashed. Although I had long ago learned to live with it, it could at times cause some discomfort; but I assured the greatly concerned doctor, that I had learned to get on with my life, and although it made me a one-footed footballer, I told him that I was better than most on one leg. I remember he smiled grimly at that piece of self-praise but said little.

22

Next my elbows and knees were tapped with a little rubber hammer making my arms and legs fly about like a newly stringed Pinocchio.

Then I was asked to drop my trousers.

Standing, slightly embarrassed, in all my glory, the medic, worryingly, slipped his hand under my testicles. He said 'cough' I thought he said 'off' and I was halfway down the corridor before he let go.

"Stop fooling around sonny, this is deadly serious."

(He could say that again, he was holding all that was dear to me in his little gnarled hand).

"Now I want you to pee in that bottle over there on the shelf."

"What from here? " I said.

"In the toilet - next door laddie" he growled, thoroughly unhappy with yet another clever dick going through his hands.

As I waddled toward the inviting bottles with my trousers still around my ankles, a vast sigh of despair emanated from the frustrated Doc.

"Pull your trousers up son you look like Donald Duck" he muttered, and added grimly "And with a very tiny beak at that."

Well it was cold in that room.

Sitting quietly with a cup of tea, awaiting dismissal, I was called into the office and informed that my deformed left ankle was not up to it, I was to be made Grade 3, and that there would be no National Service for me.

Now most young men I knew tried everything under the sun to fail their medical, but although one part of me did not want to go into the forces, the rest of me was quite looking forward to it.

"But sir, Grade 3 or not, I am as fit as a flea. I play football and cricket and swim. I'm a cross-country champion. I cannot go home and tell my father that I'm a reject."

"Sorry son, Grade 3 you are, and that's it."

I didn't tell dad.

He asked me which service I had put my name down for, and I told him that the Navy was my first choice, then the RAF, then the Army.

Father, an Army man himself, simply nodded.

"As long as you do your duty son - that's all that matters."

Big brother Lar had done his stint in the RAF at the wars end, after having served three years from the age of fifteen in the Home

Guard, and brother Colin, although four years my senior, was at that very time already in the RAF doing his National Service, having finished his studies before being called up at aged twenty-two.

About a month or so after my medical (now long forgotten), another O.H.M.S. envelope addressed to me plopped through the letterbox.

On opening it, there, as bold as brass, were the words,

'You are to report to RAF Cardington on May 10th 1956 for your National Service' and with the command, a second-class rail ticket and a couple of pages of instructions.

I was both pleased and excited, and I could tell father was pleased too, although he said nothing. He simply nodded and got on with loading his favourite pipe.

I must have been one of the very few Grade 3 lads to be called up in those days, and thanks to my pleading, that dear old humourless Medic's decision had changed my life forever.

FAST TRAIN TO CARDINGTON

May 10th 1956 was a day of significance to me for it could have easily been a much later date that I join the ranks of fighting men.

Knowing that Her Majesty would be calling for me sometime in my eighteenth year, I had applied for early call up instead of waiting my turn. The reason for my perceived eagerness was simply that every time that I applied for a job, I was politely told to try elsewhere as I would be soon leaving to do my two years in the 'mob.' I must say I did find this most unfair at the time and even wrote to the Daily Mirror about it. They of course, being the Daily Mirror, edited my letter to shreds, and made it sound as if I was a wastrel. I had ended up doing a series of unskilled 'fill in' jobs culminating in labouring on a building site, building a school in Downend. The irony of that job was that I was swiftly 'promoted' to dumper driver and given the princely wage of £14 per week. (A comparative fortune in those days)

At that time, as a fresh-faced youth, barely eighteen years old, and with the whole wide world in front of me and just waiting to be explored, I was soon to realise it was a date when Her Majesty decided, in her wisdom, to take my freedom away from me (and my £14 per week) for two years. It was the day that I was sent to RAF Cardington in Bedfordshire to join the Royal Air Force, to be kitted out, and to start my two years National Service.

There was no arguing about it, you were commanded to go - and go you did.

With my call up papers in my pocket and a change of socks in my battered old suitcase I, not without a little trepidation, boarded that hissing, aforesaid King, at Temple Meads with fathers words ringing in my ears.

"You've got to do your duty son, so you might as well do it with a good heart and enjoy it."

In what seemed like no time at all my train was at Paddington, and I was aboard the 'Recruits Special' bound for Bedfordshire. That train seemed to be full of fresh-faced kids like myself, and I realised that I would not be alone in facing what lay ahead.

A lorry awaited us at the journeys end and a friendly Sergeant ushered us aboard. On arriving at the camp he showed us to our billet, where we dumped our suitcases before he took us to the mess for our first taste of service food. We were all so hungry by now that we wolfed down every morsel of the modest fare, and some even went back for 'seconds.'

We were told to muster outside our billets at four o'clock, by which time we had been joined by many others from all parts of the British Isles.

At this point we must have looked a motley shower, all of us dressed in civvies, and mostly looking totally bewildered as we were then marched to the camp barber's shop. There must have been one hundred and twenty or more of us, and one wag commented,

'This is the longest barber's queue I've ever been in.'

He needn't have worried, it didn't take long. There were about six barbers inside and they must have thought it was a sheep-shearing contest.

Ignoring all protests, every new recruit got the same treatment, namely the old serviceman's S.B.& S (short back and sides), and when I say short I mean short. When later we were given our berets to wear, not a single hair was in sight.

Everyone on being called up made sure that that they had their hair cut reasonably short and tidy to combat the threat of the dreaded SB&S.

This they quickly found out was a total waste of time and money.

The camp 'assassin' (barber) gave everyone the same shearing.

When the job was completed (time 1 min. 30 secs. per shear) the Shearer had the temerity to charge you 1/- (a shilling) and then sneer,

'See you next week boys.'

When you placed your cap or beret on your 'swede,' to all intents and purposes you might as well have been bald.

Long gone were the old D.A.'s and Tony Curtis's.

Those pampered locks of hair made a very sad sight now, as they lay intermingled, on the 'sheep Shearer's' floor.

We now all looked the same.

The first lesson in discipline had begun. Everyone equal, and everyone treated the same. Mind you, when we were all in uniform those haircuts certainly helped to make us look a smart bunch of lads. It wasn't until you had finished basic training (square bashing) and then trade training, did the pressure on 'getting your hair cut' ease off. Even then it was a big crime to be seen with scruffy hair and one needed to keep it tidy.

During my two years in the RAF I must have had my hair cut at least fifty times and yet that very first 'shear' is the only one that I remember. It seems remarkable – but there it was.

On the very first morning of our new life we were mustered in front of the dozen or so billets still wearing our civilian clothes, and we were formed into three lines.

What followed was a very strict lecture given by a remarkably pristine Sergeant, with gleaming brass-wear and shining boots. He pre-empted his talk with the warning to 'pay attention as we would only be told the following once.'

It was pointed out (just in case we did not know) who was a Sergeant and who was a Corporal, and that they were non-commissioned officers.

That we needed to address all NCOs by their rank, and all Officers as 'sir.'

That we do not salute NCOs, and that we always salute Officers. We were told that when we salute Officers we are in effect saluting Her Majesty in the shape of the Officers badge. The Golden Eagle.

We were then told once more to listen very carefully, as we were about to be issued with our service number. That we were to memorise it, and never forget it under the threat of death. From that moment on we were told

'YOU ARE NOW NOT A NAME - YOU ARE A NUMBER.'

Your name was called out and your lifelong number issued. You then called it back slowly and loudly followed by the shout of - SERGEANT!

"NORTHAM 5019897 - SERGEANT."

I WILL NEVER FORGET IT.

I guarantee there is not one serviceman in the whole world that served in any of the armed forces who will ever forget his service number - especially his 'last three'.

In my case - '897 Northam - Sergeant.'

It was your 'last three' that was usually requested from the powers that be - especially on pay parade.

Pay parades were special, and was a greatly looked forward to event. The whole camp would gather and line up in a hangar, with the Officers and the Pay Corps members sitting at a long table in front of you. Although the Officer remained seated during the procedure, he always wore his cap with his gleaming Golden Eagle badge to the fore.

Your name would be called out in Alphabetical order, starting the first week at 'A' and the following week at 'Z'. Being an 'N' meant that I was always one of the last to be reimbursed. On hearing your name called you marched smartly up to the table, came to attention and shouted loudly your 'last three' and your name.

('897 - Northam - SIR'). You saluted, and were handed your loot (26/-) before saluting the Golden Eagle once more, about turning, and marching smartly away.

This ritual became second nature, and although a major event in itself, it ensured that everyone was paid properly and I suppose at the same time, it helped reinforce discipline.

Payday was fondly known in the RAF as 'the day the Golden Eagle shits,' due to the fact that your precious loot was dispensed from under that gleaming Golden Eagle residing on the Officers head.

Amongst the twenty or so lads in my billet (a wooden hut with two coke stoves down the centre) were a South African Boer, a frail looking vicars son from Shepton Mallet, a West Indian lad, a tall spindly son of a Lord of the Realm (whose name escapes me) and a very handsome twenty two year old Scottish lad by the name of Alex Thompson. Alex had just completed University and had studied mining engineering. On the fourth day of our ten days at Cardington, during the morning parade, the Sergeant bellowed, "Any of youse scrawny lot that plays that poofs game goff - two paces forward."

Alex alone stepped forward, whereupon the Sergeant glanced swiftly at a piece of paper he had secreted in his hand.

"You don't look too much like a poof son - what do you play orff?"

"Scratch Sergeant"

"What?" yelled the NCO.

"Scratch Sergeant - I play off scratch"

"Is that any good lad?" he enquired.

"Well Sergeant - some seem to think it is."

"Fall out laddie and report to the Commanding Officers office. Tell the sergeant there that you play orff scratch."

I never saw Alex again. When we got back to the billet his bed-space had been cleared and we heard that he spent most of his time playing golf with the C.O.

When I say that I never saw Alex again, that is not quite true.

Some ten years later, (and now a married insurance man) I was standing outside my office on The Straits at Fishponds when I noticed across the road, a familiar face talking to a gentleman. It was Alex, and although he said he could remember me, I could see that he didn't. Apparently he had married a Bristol girl and was down from Scotland visiting her family. I was pleased to see him, and at least he confirmed the story of his golfing days with the C.O.

Meanwhile my eventful ten days at Cardington carried on.

It was at Cardington that we were fully kitted out - medically checked thoroughly and were given a number of aptitude and intelligence tests.

The morning after our Intelligence test the sergeant shouted

"Brown - Northam - Smith" two paces forward. Fall out and report to the education block."

On arrival the three of us were given another series of I.Q. tests and sent on our way.

The following morning I was greeted with the bellow,

"Northam fall out and report to the education block."

Now alone, I nervously entered to be greeted by the same three Education Officers.

"Can you tell me why I am here sir?" I enquired. "I can promise you I have completed your tests to the best of my ability."

"It's nothing to worry about lad. We need you to take some other tests however, to complete our records, that's all."

I sat alone and, from memory, completed another three or four tests during the course of the morning. The officers, I do remember, were most friendly and brought me tea and a wad at the mid morning break.

Finally they began to ask questions about my family and my schooling and what dad did for a living. What I wanted to do in life etc., before finally bidding me rejoin my colleagues.

"What is this all about sir?" I enquired.

"Well airman - we are greatly puzzled. According to your test results you have an I.Q. higher than Einstein. Today was our check to see if this was so and that we had not made an error. I'm afraid there has been no error and your I.Q. is as found."

Relieved, I burst out laughing and seeing the instant hardening of the Officers faces I explained.

"You see sir, I enjoy doing those tests. They are just a bit of fun to me. The teachers at primary school used to give me pages of them to do to while away the time whilst the others caught up with me. I shouldn't read too much into that."

I must admit I was quietly pleased with what they had said, thinking to myself 'Einstein eh! Great - they will probably let me be a pilot,' and I hurried off back to join my mates.

I was very shocked a few days later when we were all gathered to hear our trade allocations, and the friendly Education Officer called out,

"Northam - Wireless Operator."

So much for Einstein's I.Q.

Although I was only at Cardington for ten days, three further happenings helped to shape my character and my view of the world.

The first makes me smile to this day when it is brought to mind.

On the second day at around 6pm, as I lay on my 'pit' pondering my new life, the billet door burst open and in strode Lord X's son, his face was a picture of anguish and total horror.

"You would not believe what I have just witnessed," he spluttered in his cultured Old Etonian accent.

"Try me m'lud," I said sympathetically.

"You will think I am making this up, but I have just been to the ablutions to swill my face and there was an oaf washing his feet in the hand basin. His feet mark you, and when he saw the look of horror on my face he simply grinned and said 'lend me your flannel m'lud I've got some dirt between my toes'. Oh Lord what have they done to me? Where have they sent me? I really will not be able to stand another 665 days of this."

Thankfully for his Lordship, the next day he (like Alex before him) disappeared. We heard later, that he had been sent to Officer training and was, no doubt, given his very own washbasin.

Perhaps not so funny was the sight, just seven days into our service life, of our vicars son, sat on his bed, fag dangling from his lips, a bottle of Brown ale on his locker, 'Bulling up' his newly acquired boots and saying "I'll never get the f...... hang of this." I don't think father would have been best pleased with his young son's awakening to the big wide world. Although on reflection it would have made a lively sermon on a Sunday morning. The only things missing, were a betting slip and a pretty young thing sprawled invitingly on his bed.

Definitely not so funny was the next occurrence.

The South African - a six foot squarely built individual with a

Bull-like neck - had from day one persisted in taunting the West Indian lad who slept opposite him, who, to his credit, said little and got on with the job in hand.

This particular evening, we were all sat on our beds laughing and joking as we tried to burn the pimples off our boot toecaps with a spoon handle heated by holding it over a candle before meticulously rubbing boot polish, liberally mixed with spit, in tiny circles on the now flattened leather, in a bid to form a hard shiny crust of gleaming black and ending up with boots the equal of the NCOs.

All the while the big Boer got more and more insulting toward our black comrade.

"Hey matey - pack it in" I said eventually, "Leave the lad alone. We are all in the same boat, so let's all row together."

"What's it to you Englishman?" he growled "It's between the Kaffir and me."

"It isn't when your incessant diatribe in that crap accent of yours starts grating on my ears - so knock it in the head."

"I'll knock you in the head Englishman," said Transvaal Ted, and he got up and came at me nostrils flaring.

Now he was a big powerful boy, and I could see that it would be doubtful if I could see him off, and he obviously meant business.

As I stood, he lunged and swung a punch at my head, which I evaded, and as he passed me I managed to get him around the neck and using his weight and momentum swung him to the ground landing between two beds with me on top of him. In an instant I heard a metallic click and realised that he was holding a lethal looking flick knife dangerously close to my throat.

"Get off of me Englishman," he hissed "Or I will spill your blood."

I wasn't going to argue with piece of sharp Sheffield steel, and gingerly got to my feet.

The West Indian was busily polishing his toecaps. He wasn't about to help me. Our Springbok pal, although still angry and still clutching his knife, pointed at the black lad and blurted out.

"See my brave English friend, he would have let you die rather than defend you." Which was patently obvious.

"Maybe so" I said, "But there's no need to taunt him. He's no different than you or I."

"Have you got a sister?" asked the Boer. "Cos if you have, would you feel the same if she married him?"

Brave fool I might be, but hypocrite I am not, and I said no more.

Reaching out his hand, now in reconciliation, the South African shook mine saying, pointing to the floor space between the beds,

"Fair play Englishman, you almost had me for a moment back there."

After we left Cardington I never saw the man again.

Wrong as he was, our little skirmish taught me another valuable lesson in life.

Despite the medicals and intelligence tests, the main reason for being at Cardington was to be kitted out with your uniform, and for the record the kit you were issued with is listed below.

This was it. Should you lose any of it, or wear it out, you were expected to replace it yourself. Although there was some petty theft amongst the recruits, by and large there was an unwritten law that you looked after one another, and such occurrences were rare and definitely not tolerated. Thieves were severely dealt with.

You were issued with: -

A Dress Uniform, which had a belted jacket with brass buttons, plus a Peaked Cap, which carried the distinctive brass RAF badge.

One Working Uniform, (i.e.) Trousers and Bomber Jacket.

One Beret with Brass Badge.

One Greatcoat with brass buttons.

Three collarless Blue Shirts with separate collars.

One set of Collar Studs.

Three Vests - Three pairs of Underpants.

Three pairs of thick Woollen Socks.

Two pairs of Pyjamas.

One pair of Gym Shorts.

Two Towels.

One pair of Boots - One pair of Shoes - One pair of Plimsolls.

One Black Tie - One pair of Woollen Gloves.

One pair of Braces.

One Webbing Belt.

One pair of Denims (boiler suit).

One Wet Weather Cape (poncho).

One Kit Bag.

One Shoulder Bag.

Sewing Kit ('housewife') consisting of needles, wool, and cotton.

Two Shoe Brushes and a Button Cleaner.

Knife Fork and Spoon (your 'irons') stamped with your service number.

YOUNG WARRIORS

Cyril Andrews – Malcolm Bell – The Author – Obadiah Davies
Keeping RAF Hednesford safe from attackers 1956

THE DRILL INSTRUCTORS

Corporals Rolfe, Bristowe and Watson

LOOKING FITTER

Midway through 'Square Bashing' at Hednesford

Back Row left to right – Malcolm Bell, The Author, Tony Moss
Front Row left to right – ?, Cyril Andrews and Obe Davies

A PAIR OF CONFIDENT ERKIES

THAT WEBBING BELT
NEEDS CLEANING

Malcolm Bell and the Author
taking a break outside their Billet
at RAF Hednesford 1956

The Author at RAF Hednesford 1956

W.O.P. 30. RAF COMPTON BASSETT

Fred Nurk six from left back row with T.T. rider far right
Middle row. - Jock Miller second from left - 'Wally` Wareham last but one
The Author middle bottom row

SPIC AND SPAN

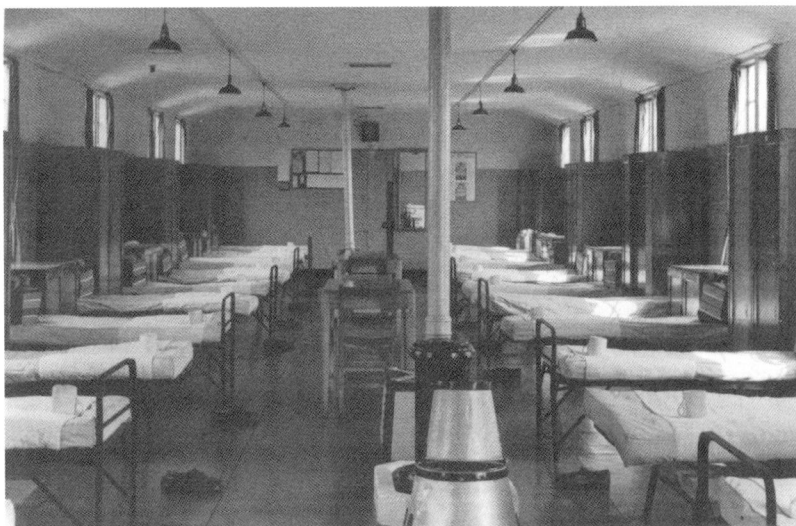

Hednesford billet laid out for inspection

NINE STONE WEAKLING

OH! I DO LIKE YOU

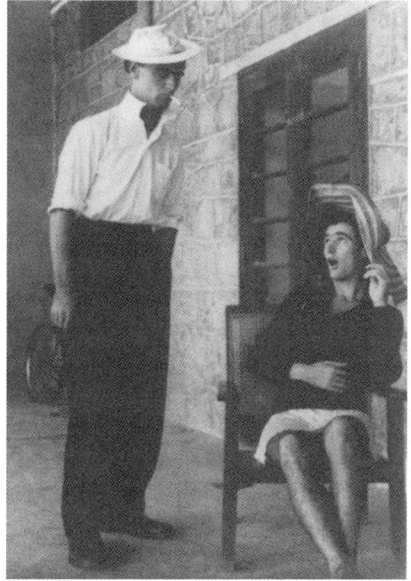

The author six weeks into Aden tour -
sixteen pounds lighter than when he
arrived -

Standing outside his billet door with
Block Four in the background.

The author chatting up his alter ego
on the veranda Block Five Bottom West

THE PENTAGONS

Front Row Left to right – Bobbie Campbell   Margaret Sowerby   Fred Nurk
Back Row Left to Right – The Author and Rod Hamill

PENTAGONS DEBUT

The Pentagons first show at the Families Club Khormaksar
From left to right - Rod Hamill, Fred Nurk, Bruce Nash, The Author
and Margaret Sowerby on guitar

SWINGING

TRIO IN SONG

Rod Hamill, Margaret Sowerby and
the Author after rehearsal
in the Airman's Club

The Author, Margaret Sowerby
and Fred Nurk rehearsing.
At the Airman's Club
On dais before the stage was built

SANDSTORM APPROACHING

An amazing photograph taken from the top of Block Five
moments before a sandstorm struck.
This one lasted for a day and a half.

BARELY A DROP TO DRINK

The Author, Fred Nurk and Bobbie Campbell
Alongside a very small water hole in the middle of the desert
(A few miles from Sheik Othman)

TAXI SIR!

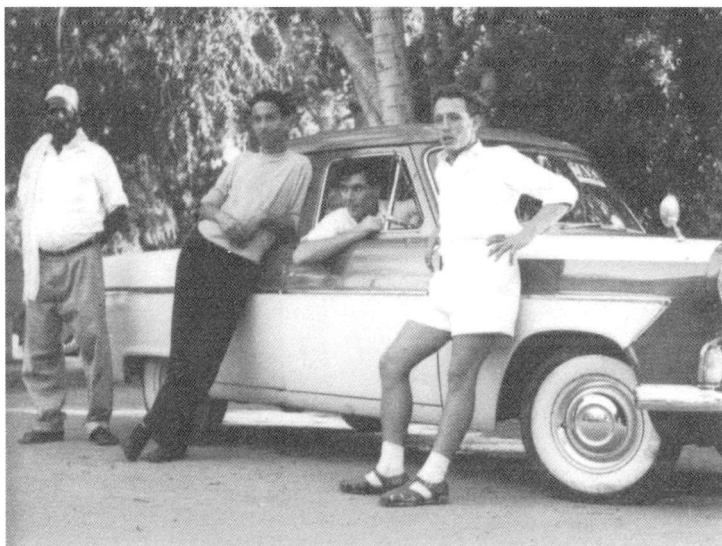

Fred, the Author and Bobbie posing at the Oasis in Sheik Othman
having commandeered the poor Arab's Taxi

A PRETTY YOUNG ADEN LADY

The Author with an inquisitive young Arab girl.
Sheik Othman Oasis

MISS YEMEN

The author as Miss Yemen in the Miss Aden Protectorate
Competition, held at Khormaksar airport
He came last!

MISS SHEIK OTHMAN

Fred Nurk as the Oasis Queen
in the same Competition.
He came second!

MISS MAALA

Rod Hamill as Miss Maala
(My favourite to win it)
She came last but one despite trying to
bribe the judges with her 'favours'

A Pint Size China Mug.

This was your kit and provided everything you needed to survive.

Once a week you had to lay it out on your bed in a specific order for inspection and Lord help you if it wasn't pristine clean and that there was anything missing.

You were also issued with an identity card and a small Pass Book with all your personal details on it.

On the last day of our ten days at RAF Cardington we all attended a big dance held in the enormous hangar built to house the ill fated Airship R101.

I remember some of the new recruits being invited up on stage to join the ten-piece dance band; others eagerly grabbed the mike and sang. I also recall that some of them were very good, in particular a trumpeter, a young lad of exceptional ability, and I thought that some of them just might become famous one day. Perhaps they did.

For me, just being in that hangar I felt that I had experienced a little bit of history that day, and could imagine myself back in the past standing alongside all those excited people as they gazed in awe at the giant new form of transport floating before them.

My first ten days as a raw RAF recruit was an eye opening experience for a young lad and although I didn't appreciate it at the time I now realise what a life enhancing adventure it had been.

Most of all though, my ten days at Cardington saw a fresh faced country boy grow considerably in stature on the long road to manhood.

I WILL MAKE A MAN OF YOU IN EIGHT WEEKS

Fully kitted out and with the prospect of being a Wireless Operator for Her Majesty for the best part of my two years, I was bundled onto a train once more, but this time heading North West for Shropshire, and RAF Hednesford, where I was firstly to do my basic training ('square bashing'). The Morse Code was to come later.

The lorries were once again waiting for us when we arrived. We were all clad in our sparkling new uniforms and wearing our smart new peaked caps. We each carried our kit bags, now crammed full with our second uniform - boots - irons - denims and the like.

Beside each lorry stood an immaculately turned out Corporal with gleaming boots, immaculately Blancoed webbing belt, and shining brass-wear. Their caps were shaped with much use and the peaks instead of jutting forward, as was ours, fell down their foreheads to rest upon their eyebrows. They looked a tough and frightening bunch.

Their look was not the half of it. As one, they began to bellow.

"Jump to it you scrawny bunch."

"Smarten up - you're in the RAF now, not idling about in Civvy Street.

MOVE - MOVE - MOVE."

Terrified we all began milling around not knowing quite where to move.

"Get that kit and your scrawny selves on that lorry - and fast - jump to it you stupid idle bunch of nincompoops. Move - when I say move – MOVE. Jump to it man" yelled this aggressive terror, into the trembling ear of the poor lad nearest to him.

"Move man, or I'll have your guts for garters. What's your name laddie?" "Goodfellow" stuttered the terrified lad.

"Goodfellow - Goodfellow! I'll tell you whether you're a good fellow lad. And when you address me it's Corporal d'you understand?

So what's your name?"

"Goodfellow – Corporal."

"That's better. - Last three?"

"Sorry Corporal?"

34

"Last three - what' s your last three?"

"I'm sorry Corporal I don't understand."

"Right, you're for the guardroom when we get to camp.

Forgotten your number already. You are no longer a good fellow - you're a number. But in your case as you have forgotten yours, you're a TWAT. What are you?"

"A Twat Corporal."

"A WHAT?"

"I'm a twat Corporal."

"Louder"

"I'M A TWAT CORPORAL," said the poor sole now shaking like a leaf.

"There you are then. You've got no number and you ain't a Goodfellow - you're a TWAT. And don't you forget that." he screamed.

The poor lad was near to tears, and we were terrified that he was going to pick on us next.

"Don't just stand there get on that friggin lorry - MOVE - MOVE - MOVE."

Chaos ensued as young men - now scared out of their wits - tried to climb over one another to do this half-human's bidding.

Noting the futility of the scrimmage I stood back to allow things to clear.

It was of course a big mistake.

In no time I found the apoplectic drill instructor (for that's what he turned out to be) standing inches in front of me with his bulging eyes glaring into mine and his halitosis breath snorting up my nostrils.

"Are you deaf pretty boy? When I say jump you bloody well jump - now get your arse onto the back of that lorry or I'll kick it from here to town."

"How do you suggest I circumvent the milling bodies of my colleagues - Corporal?" I enquired.

"Colleagues - colleagues! They're scum that's what they are. They ain't got half a brain between the lot of 'em. Look at 'em they're a bloody rabble - that's what they are, a bloody rabble, and I'll bet they've all forgotten their bloody numbers."

Leaving me he wheeled on the scrabbling mass shouting (no, not shouting - screaming)

"JUMP TO IT - JUMP TO IT - ON - ON - ON - MOVE – MOVE - MOVE - MOVE."

It worked. Suddenly I was left alone to lob my kit bag aboard, and swiftly join it.

"See that - see that you stupid nincompoops. Pretty boy's done it in one."

The tailgate was swung up and secured, and the lorry roared off to doom.

Through the main gates of RAF Hednesford the lorries roared, passing the Spitfire and Meteor standing proudly on guard, and screeched to a jolting holt, stopping with their backs set at a 45 degree angle to the large area of neatly manicured grass that fronted the imposing guardhouse. Almost before the lorries had halted, that terrifying, screaming Corporal had the tailgate down bellowing "OFF - OFF - OFF - JUMP TO IT - OFF - OFF - OFF."

If there was panic at the station it was nothing to the panic now.

Luckily being last on I was first off and I swung my kit bag and myself neatly around the lorries side whilst my travelling companions disintegrated into a teeming mass of kit bags and bodies. It looked like Lemmings piling over a cliff.

All the while the air was rent with "OFF - OFF - OFF - JUMP - JUMP - JUMP - MOVE - MOVE - MOVE."

Finally the lorry was empty and sped off leaving the screaming Corporal - now in his element - yelling at the top of his voice.

"Into line you useless shower - three lines - leave your kit bags where they are. MOVE - MOVE - MOVE."

The writhing mass scuttled about valiantly trying to obey the bellowing horror.

At this moment the D.I. noticed a weedy sickly looking recruit standing forlornly without his cap.

"Where's your bloody headgear Airman you 'orrible little weed? You know the rules - headgear to be worn at all times - where is it? - Where is it? Have you lost it? 'Cos if you 'ave d'you know the penalty for losing Her Majesties equipment? Well do you? Well I will tell you Airman - two years in the bloody Glasshouse that's what. And when you get out of there you'll still have to do your two years. You matey boy ain't never going to get out of the mob, you'll be in it forever. Now where's your bloody lid?"

The D.I.'s diatribe had been spat out with him hardly drawing a breath, and certainly giving his young victim no time at all to reply to his constant enquiries about the fate of his hat.

The poor Erkie, grey with fear and trembling with terror, tried to speak but no words came out.

"Speak up you little runt or I'll 'ave you in the Glasshouse now – and I'll see to it that you never come out. Nobody - nobody ruins my parade without his hat, so speak up - where's your bloody cap?"

The trembling Erkie, not able to speak, pointed to the middle of the lawn where a brand new cap - badge shining in the sun - lay blissfully unaware of the problems it had caused.

As the poor young Airman had scrambled to get out of the truck someone had accidentally knocked his cap off which had then cartwheeled to the centre of the lawn.

"Get that bloody cap on lad this minute" bellowed the Corporal.

As the lad left his place in the line to fetch the wayward cap a terrifying shout came from the Guardroom door as a military policeman yelled

"GET OFF THAT BLOODY GRASS YOU IMBECILE - UNLESS YOU'RE A GOAT.

ONLY GOATS ARE ALLOWED ON MY GRASS."

What a dilemma.

Two years in the Glasshouse for not having a cap, or God knows how long in the Guardroom for standing on the grass.

Catch 22 indeed.

The shell-shocked young Airman decided that the Guardroom was the better option, and scurried across the grass like a scolded ferret. Everyone waited for the sword of Damocles to fall, but the lad had chosen well and he was allowed to become reunited with his cap.

By now of course we were all totally aware of what lay in store for us, and, unbeknown at that moment - it was not to get any better.

"Youse lot 'ave got a lot to learn and I'm here to teach youse. As sure as my name's Corporal Watson I will make a man of all of youse in eight weeks."

We were all lined up in three lines, and the drill instructors paced up and down in front of us spitting out rules and regulations as fast as a Bren-gun spat out lead. Nine parts of it flew over my head and I hoped and prayed that some of my new mates were taking it in.

Then came our next ordeal.

We were introduced to our Sergeant, one Sergeant Moore, who marched out in front of us gleaming like a new shilling. The gleaming Sergeant had his own special way of speaking the Queen's English. His ability to torture vowels was quite unique.

"Git a goo'eod luka at me loovely boo-iys 'cos this h'is how I expect you'a to turn hout on parade every morning. Smaart as paint - smaart as paint I say - smaaaart as paint. Right then, now you'a knowa me h'I want to know you'a. From the right - froont rank first - h'I want you'a to shoout hout your'a name and number. H'I want you'a to be heard h'and h'I want you to finish it hoff with 'Sergeant'."

Pointing his swagger stick he bellowed, "Start."

Down the line we went calling name and number. I was standing in the back row and therefore one of the last to sound off, and the bloke next to me whispered, "Bugger - I've forgotten mine."

"Make one up mate, he wont know," I muttered.

Luckily, for a man whose memory can be dodgy, I had mine fixed.

"5019897 Northam - Sergeant" I shouted confidently.

The lad next to me shouted "6598691 – Jackson - Sergeant."

"Stop," yelled the Sergeant. "What's yoo'a number Jackson?"

"6287419 - Sergeant."

"You nincompoop, did you think you'a could fool me Jackson - you'a on a fizzer Airman. Take his real name and number Corporal."

Later the unfortunate Jackson asked me how the Sergeant had caught him, and was totally bewildered when I told him,

"Cos we are all 5019's you pillock - except the regulars who are 268's."

He still didn't 'twig' it.

AND SO IT BEGINS

There were 120 of us making up our flight, (Flight 7 – B Squadron) and it was this happy band that were to be 'made men of.' Most of us were eighteen year olds and barely wet behind the ears, but amongst us were a few older lads of around twenty-one who had just finished their apprenticeships or University.

A small number of the lads had signed on for extra service, usually three years instead of the statutory two, but occasionally for nine. These lads were now deemed as 'regulars' and were paid a great deal more than us conscripts.

We were, seemingly willy-nilly, bundled into six billets that had an ablutions block alongside that serviced all the huts. The ablutions block contained ample showers, toilets and hand basins to accommodate the flight, and there was always plenty of hot water.

Shuffling into our new home, we all flopped down on the nearest vacant bed - every one of us both mentally and physically drained.

Our peace lasted but five minutes. The door burst open and Corporal Watson was upon us again.

"On your feet and stand by your beds," he bellowed.

"Every time an NCO or an Officer comes through this door you leap to your feet and stand by your beds immediately, and it doesn't matter what state of dress you are in."

Turning to a trembling pale youth from Hampshire he said,

"In your case pretty boy I shall look forward to seeing you in your nightie."

He then walked slowly up and down the billet, (ours was Hut 66), studying each of us in turn, swagger stick under his arm and eyes peering out from under his cap peak, which came down almost to the bridge of his nose. All his kit gleamed.

His Blancoed webbing belt with its gleaming brass buckle was tightly clasped around his waist, exaggerating the size of his chest. And his boots shone like glass.

He was immaculate and he looked very intimidating.

"Wellington where are you?" he said at last.

"Sir," said a tall studious looking lad.

"Corporal -sonny Jim - Corporal. See these stripes laddie - I'm a bloody Corporal not an Officer. Youse are going to get to hate both those stripes and me by the time I finish with youse all. Youse had all better quickly learn to tell the difference between an NCO and an Officer, 'cos you salute Officers and quake when you see NCOs."

Bloody hell - what was happening?

What happened to civilization and democracy?

"Right Wellington, this might be your Waterloo 'cos I'm putting you in charge of this crummy lot. I understand you've been to H'university is that right?"

"Yes Sir - eh - Corporal."

"Then youse 'ave got some brains then ain't you?"

"Yes corporal - well so they say."

"Right then, youse in charge of this billet, and if it's not kept up to scratch youse to blame - ain't youse - brain-box?"

Turning to the lad with his kit on the bed next to the door, he turfed it onto the floor and said,

"You change places with brain-box - now!"

The two lads swapped places and the Corporal left.

Poor old 'Brain-box' (the name stuck) he was the last lad to be a leader of men, but with a bit of support from a couple of us he got through his eight weeks pretty much unscathed.

Soon after the Corporal had departed, and before I had time to introduce myself to my new billet mates, I went out to the ablutions block that stood in between the huts, and on returning to my nineteen new mates I said cheerfully,

"It's pissing down with rain s'no," which brought absolute silence before a Brummy accent said,

"Make up your mind pal. Is it raining or is it snowing?"

Everyone roared with laughter, and we all began to chatter away in our regional accents as we introduced ourselves, and commiserated with one another on the situation we found ourselves in. We all agreed there and then, that we were all in the same boat together, and that we needed to look to one another to get ourselves through this new ordeal.

Breakfast was at 7am and we had to be on parade at 8am. This meant an early rise if we wanted to eat and (as it very soon turned out) with the amount of exercise they put us through we were going to need that breakfast. There was always plenty of grub to start the day - eggs and bacon, fried bread, baked beans, loads of bread and of course as much tea as you could drink (Bromide laced as it was).

Lunch was usually at midday and the evening meal at six. The food was pretty basic, but there was usually plenty of it once you got used to it. It was served cafeteria style with the cooks slopping a spoonful of the days fare on your plate as you filed by clutching your mug and your irons for dear life. There were rarely any 'seconds' although (if you could stand the taste of Bromide) there was always plenty of tea that you drew from a row of chrome urns set on the side of the mess. The cooks tried to vary the menu, but there was no choice - take it or leave it was the dish of the day, so if there was something you didn't like you either ate it or starved. I very quickly learnt to eat most things. There was always the NAAFI (Navy, Army Air Force Institute) on camp where you could get a snack if you were desperate.

Although the food in the NAAFI was very cheap, it still cost, and with only 26/- per week to play with, I learned to eat cookhouse fare.

The NAAFI was an amazing place and combined everything a young serviceman could want. In the evening you could relax there playing snooker or table tennis or darts or what ever you wanted, from chess to cards. There was a bar where the price of beer was very low. There was also a little cafeteria where you could get a cheap plateful of egg and chips etc. During the day there was a substantial shop that sold everything for your needs, such as cotton - Blanco (for your webbing belt) Brasso for your buttons, wool to darn your socks, writing paper and stamps, all at knock down prices.

The original super market I suppose.

The first week of our eight was taken up mostly with teaching us drill. We were continually made to line up making a straight line by looking to our left ('left dress') thrusting our left arm out to reach the next man's shoulder and shuffling (if need be) to get ourselves straight.

We were taught how to march together - how to carry our rifle - how to salute, and most of all how to halt when commanded. It was gruelling work and many of the less fit lads struggled. Looking back I can see why we frustrated our instructors, and why every (even the slightest) error had the culprit doing 20 press-ups.

We must have looked an ill disciplined rabble. And largely unfit. Those early morning inspections became a nightmare for some. As we stood in our three lines the gleaming Sergeant Moore strode slowly up and down - his eyes everywhere. He found something wrong with everyone. If the whim took him he would bark out a stream of insults, and then make the poor recipient drop to the floor for the compulsory press-ups. If he was unhappy with the way you did your press ups, he would bellow out "Rubbish - Do fouwa – mouwa."

Sergeant Moore and his 'fouwa - mouwa' became something of a joke amongst us recruits, and every time he would shout it, a very silent titter would go through the ranks.

I can tell you there was more Blanco and Brasso and Boot Polish (the dreaded three 'bees') used amongst our terrified bunch than in the whole of the British Army.

About 10 days into our training, during Sergeant Moore's eagle eyed scrutiny, he stopped at this rather swarthy looking lad who happened to sleep two beds down from me in our billet. He had told us that his name was Joseph and was immediately nicknamed Gypsy Joe. He was a very introverted lad who did not want to make friends with anyone, and kept himself very much to himself.

The Sergeant started to shout and scream at the lad.

"You dirty filthy individual, you'as collar's manky. You'as shirt's manky, you'as manky. You'as lousy, you filthy oaf. Have you'a washed today? Have you'a washed since you 'ave been here? You'a stink you'a lousy individual. Fouwa paces forward and aboout turn."

The poor lad was now standing squarely in front of us all and was obviously ill at ease. The Sergeant then firstly made him take off his beret before shouting "You 'ave got fleas you'a manky Airman - fleas. Youse will give us all fleas you'a lousy crummy man."

The irate NCO then proceeded to make Joe undress, one piece of clothing at a time, and as each piece of uniform was discarded it was held up at arms length on the end of the Sergeants swagger stick, to the near hysterical screams of,

"Loook at this. You'a filthy scum, you'a aven't washed since you'a ave been here. You're lousy - blooody lousy. You're a disgrace to yourself - your mates and to the Royal Air Force."

Eventually Gypsy Joe was down to his underpants, his socks being the last items to be discarded. His swarthy skin did look as though he hadn't had a wash; in fact I seem to remember he almost shone a peculiar bronze-like colour in the late May sunshine.

"Right you'a lousy Airman, pick up you'as gear and carry it to the bathhouse."

He then called four men forward to accompany him with the instructions to scrub him down with carbolic soap, using scrubbing brushes. Corporal Watson was sent along to supervise, with the instruction for his clothes to be dumped in a bath along with a lot more carbolic.

Later that evening the humiliated Gypsy Joe, now (I must admit) looking sparkling fresh, was sitting alone in the NAAFI. He looked so forlorn I went across and sat down beside him.

"Come on Joe" I said, "We are all in this together. What's it all about?"

He told me that he was indeed a Gypsy, and that when he joined up he couldn't believe all the clothes he had been given, and genuinely thought he had to keep his spares for the time when the ones he was wearing wore out. The poor lad could barely read or write and had hardly attended school. He was so bewildered to be amongst so many strangers and in such an alien environment. I reassured him that we were all as bemused as he was, and he was to ask any of us for help if he needed guidance.

He became a genuine hardworking recruit thereafter, although he never really lost that insular attitude. What happened to him in later life I can only guess? But I liked him. He should never have been put in the RAF in the first place, as he would have made a good soldier. Having said that, I understand he was sent to the RAF Regiment straight after square bashing, so perhaps the powers that be knew what they were doing after all.

Many friends were made during my two years but in the short eight weeks that I was doing my basic training my close pal was a Geordie lad called Malcolm Bell.

We got on well and we enjoyed the same sense of humour (when we could discern what either of us were saying).

We both thought Jackie Milburn was God.

BROKEN - SKEWERED AND GASSED

I was lucky because, what with my sport and way of life, I was pretty fit before I went into the mob, but others (many grossly over weight) being naturally lazy individuals, found all of this intense physical exercise a rude awakening. It didn't, however, stop our Corporal Watson from picking on me, which he did daily. Perhaps he could read my mind, for although I did everything asked to the best of my ability, I couldn't help thinking that Corporal Watson was a completely thick ignoramus. Maybe he was, but on reflection I doubt it. I now realise what he was all about. He was doing a job, and what's more he was very good at it. He had had literally thousands of men through his hands and he must have met many like me, fools, who were determined to 'buck the system', and he was determined to break me.

As I said before, I suppose 75% of our eight weeks training was spent 'Square Bashing.'

Marching up and down, rifles on our shoulders, learning how to keep in time with your colleagues. But initially you were taught how to obey an order - instantly - no questions asked - do it.

We were inspected every morning on muster parade, and heaven help you if your buttons, cap badge and webbing weren't gleaming and your boots shining like glass. Your trousers pressed and shirt and collar immaculate. Your hair had to be regulation SB&S and you had to have at least 1/3d (one shilling and three pence) on your person at all times along with your identity card. The money was in case you were required to 'Get your hair cut' (one shilling) or you needed to write home (stamp 3d).

After the first week we were given a rifle to drill with.

I got to know that Lee Enfield well, especially when Corporal Watson decided (once again) to make an example of me on the vast parade ground.

"Fall out Northam" he yelled, and marching up to within an inch of my face, began spitting (literally) expletives about my drill technique, my ancestry et al. I (motionless), barely containing my anger, simply stared into his eyes saying to myself (and he knew what I was thinking),

'You stupid - ignorant - pea brained twat.'

"Right laddie if that's the way you want it (he must have been a mind reader) get that rifle over your head and run around the square."

That square was vast, and it must have been best part of a mile around the perimeter, and that Lee Enfield weighed 9 1/2 lb.

But I was fit, and he was an ignorant twat, so off I set at the jog.

By half-way my arms were screaming, but goaded by the distant yells of,

"Get it up higher Airman," I battled on.

Approaching the gloating D.I. (exhausted as I was) I straightened up a bit and put a grim smile on my face.

"Oh youse like it Airman do you? Then go round again."

It took ten minutes or more this time, with my arms screaming for relief - but he wasn't going to beat me - was he?

So, I desperately tried to raise the gun, and equally desperately tried to smile as I approached this inflictor of cruelty at the end of my second circuit.

"Enjoying it eh Airman? Round you go again then."

The bastard!

This time I was barely able to walk never mind jog, and I had to rest my rifle across my shoulders, as I couldn't feel my arms. Sweat poured down my face as I looked up to see that the NAAFI van had arrived, and the lads were lying on the grass drinking tea and eating a bacon wad.

Believe it or not, it was only then it dawned on me - me with a supposed I.Q. higher than Einstein - I wasn't a hero - I was an idiot.

My mates didn't think I was a hero - they thought I was a fool.

This time round I didn't smile and the corporal allowed me to join the ranks, which was just as well as I was on the point of collapse. My mates quickly got me a drink as I lay on the grass exhausted. I could barely march when drill resumed, but this time I was not chastised – there was no need to.

Corporal Watson knew he had broken me - and he had.

A few days prior to my ordeal of running around the square, Watson had dragged me out in front of the lads and made me hold my rifle out to the side of me, shoulder height holding the barrel in my hand. He demonstrated how it was done first of all, and then challenged me to do it better. Of course I couldn't. I don't think that I kept it up there for a couple of minutes. There is no doubt that in trying to beat the man I had strained my arm to the degree that for a day or so I could barely hold my knife to eat, as my hand trembled uncontrollably. What I hadn't twigged was that he was holding his rifle barrel half way down with the barrel tip resting under his forearm, and not holding it right at the end like me.

He had me another day too when we were doing 'live' enemy bayonet attacks.

A small trench had been fashioned at the foot of a fairly steep forty-foot high hillock. Five of my fellow recruits were positioned at the top of the hillock and hidden from view. I was put into the trench and given a clip of five blanks, and they were told to 'fix bayonets' and to charge my trench on command. I was told to 'shoot' them as they came and they were to drop when indicated that they were shot. If they made it to the trench they were to bayonet me. Hardly fair I thought, and so I fixed my bayonet.

"What the hell are you doing Airman?" yelled Watson.

"Just a back-up Corporal" I said, "You know me - bracers and belt."

"You bloody clever dick. Youse better get it right or you're a dead Airman."

At the command 'charge' my five screaming mates jumped up and started charging down the hill toward me.

I nailed the first (metaphorically speaking) before he was hardly on his feet having already rammed one up the breach unbeknown to Watson. Number two followed tout suite, as did number three. Then disaster, my bolt action jammed and I was faced with two terrified mates hell bent on skewering me. In a flash I was on my feet out of the trench and charging straight at them, my bayonet glinting in the sun.

"Halt-Halt-Halt" screamed both Corporals and the Sergeant together, and fortunately all three of us instinctively obeyed.

(At least that proved that the training was working).

My adrenalin pumping I sucked in a deep breath, only to get the biggest bollocking of my life, culminating with being put on a 252 (charge) for disobeying orders.

To this day I do not know what I did wrong.

For whatever reason, no one else was put through that ordeal - which I suppose was just as well. The 'charge of the bayoneted Erkies' was called off immediately, and we were all led back to our much-skewered dummies for some less life threatening practice.

For me, I am glad that I went through that experience, frightening as it was, at least I could appreciate how those brave Red Coated lads at Rorke's Drift must have felt faced with 4000 Assegai wielding

Zulus bearing down on them. I only had five to contend with.

One of the most unpleasant things they forced us to do whilst teaching us to be 'fighting men', was an experience I would not wish to repeat.

We were taken to a hut far from the billets and told to don a rather cumbersome mask before entering said hut in groups of three. The NCO then threw a canister of tear gas inside and locked the door.

"Can you all breathe?" he yelled.

Then he said the stupidest of things:

"If you can't - bang on the door."

Bang on the door! If you couldn't breathe you'd be dead wouldn't you!

We were then told to take our masks off and stay put for a minute before he opened the door and let you out to fresh air and freedom.

Now I have always suffered from claustrophobia and I wasn't looking forward to this little episode in my training. However, I had little time to ponder my fate, as I was one of the second three in, and frankly shitting myself.

"Can you all breathe?" came the yell as the acrid smoke curled around us, for a split second my mind was at Auschwitz - and how I hated those bloody Nazis.

What a way to die.

"Masks off" came the shout.

Bugger that mate - I kept mine on until I heard the rattle of the door handle when only then I ripped it off to be overcome with the putrid smoke. Coughing and spluttering the three of us staggered out to fall prostrate on the grass, eyes running and stomach retching, and I only had had barely 10 seconds of the stuff. It did not matter, I got the message, and if I were you, I would keep well away from it if you can.

Brief as our introduction was to this toxic poison, the foul smell clung to our clothes, and few of us enjoyed our dinner that day, as everything tasted of chemical.

A Home From Home

Life in our billet was character building for an eighteen year old.

To start with you were away from the comfort and protection of your home and family. You were sleeping alongside a group of lads your own age and from all parts of the U.K., and from all walks of life. You learned very quickly that if you did not all pull together, you all sank together. There was no room for spoilt brats here. The weaker characters amongst us were initially helped, but they too had to learn fast, to grow up and be strong. That aside, young men (mostly unconsciously) manoeuvred to establish a 'pecking order' amongst themselves, but surprisingly, this aspect of billet life seemed to resolve itself quickly. On reflection this was probably because of the sink or swim situation we all found ourselves in, and there was no doubt that we all needed one another for most of the time. The D.I.'s made sure of that. In fact I can now see that this was an integral part of disciplining us. However there were one or two incidents that arose during those fateful weeks.

We had a lad from Yorkshire (Sheffield I seem to remember) by the name of Graham Fleetwood who was a coal miner. He was only about 5ft 6ins or 5ft 7ins tall but my goodness was he powerfully built and strong as a lion with it.

The poor lad was not the brightest light on the Christmas tree, and was deeply in love with his very pretty young beau back home. This young lady caused him much distress. Twice he disappeared from camp AWOL, and twice he was brought back to camp in the 'Snowdrops' cart. He wasn't put in 'the slammer' but was given (each time) five days 'Jankers'

That second spell of jankers I shared with him, having been put 'on a fizzer' (a 252) for my indiscretion (?) when on manoeuvres. This punishment meant that you had to report to the Guardroom in full kit at 6:30am. You were lined up and inspected by the duty Officer who would put you on another 'fizzer' if you were not immaculately turned out. You then stood to attention for ages until the camp bugler sounded Reveille and the flag was raised. You were then given mundane tasks to perform for an hour (I seemed to find myself in the cookhouse drying plates or cutting eyes out of potatoes). You were then released for normal daytime duties before having to report again to the Guardroom at 6pm. This time, following another vigorous inspection by the duty Officer, you lined up to be allocated your jobs for the next three hours by the Snowdrops. The evening jobs were designed to create as much boredom as possible (although I never saw anyone paint the coal heap white) and consisted mainly of repetitive cleaning and polishing. It didn't bother me as I could use this time as my pondering time, and the three hours usually wizzed by.

It seemed to me that the 'Snowdrops' took a great delight in humiliating Fleetwood. They would hand out their crummy little jobs - which included the 'cushy' job of cleaning and polishing the large brass bell that hung at the Guardroom door - always keeping poor old Fleetwood until last. He was then given a tiny bit of Duraglit and smirkingly told to clean the urinal with it. After the third evening, as we walked back to the billet, I said to Fleetwood - who had taken to me as I had concocted a few love letters for him to impress the love of his life, and which he would carefully copy out in his colliers hand.

"I wouldn't put up with that if that were me. He gives you the worst job every night. They are taking the micky and laughing like a drain about it. If he did that to me I would clock him one."

It was of course, just an eighteen year olds bravado talk, and I'd forgotten poor old Fleetwood thought that I was the font of all knowledge.

The next evening as the jobs were handed out the Corporal stepped forward proffering his bit of Duraglit.

"Fleetwood - clean the urinal."

In a flash a heavy miners fist swung out landing smack on the leering NCO's nose with such force that he, literally, flew across the Guardroom - struck the wall before sinking ever so slowly to the floor - blood everywhere.

There was absolute silence for a moment save for a low moan from the heavily bloodied Corporal. As we all stood to attention alongside the grim looking Fleetwood, to everyone's amazement and disbelief the Sergeant 'Snowdrop' said,

"Alright Fleetwood you can clean the bell tonight."

And we were dismissed to do our duties.

Incredibly, nothing was said or done to Fleetwood. By rights he should have got six months in the Glasshouse for striking an NCO, but he never did.

On my first six o'clock parade, the duty Officer decided to use me as his example to underline his authority, and he decided that I had missed a few bristles and needed another shave. I was given a razor (which the 'Snowdrops conveniently had to hand) and marched by a Corporal to the toilets at the back of the Guardroom and told to 'shave properly.' Lathering up with a piece of carbolic and using my fingers for a brush, I shaved under the close scrutiny of the NCO, and returned to the ranks to be once again 'inspected.'

"You have done nothing to improve your condition laddie. Go out and shave properly," directed this cruel young Officer, whose eyesight must have been appalling. Marched out again I did my best to find a bristle or two before being brought back.

"Corporal is this man disobeying orders? It looks to me as though he has done nothing to rectify his appalling scruffy state. Take him out again."

Once more I was marched to the washbasin. By now my face was red raw and I felt as though I had no skin on my cheeks and chin. This dreadful pantomime was repeated a further three times until the Corporal took pity on me and said "Take the razor blade out son - lather up and simply scrape the soap away. He's coming in this time, he won't notice that there's no blade."

For a second or two I wondered if I was being set up, but looking into the Snowdrops eyes I could see he was genuine enough. I did as he suggested, and just in time hid the blade before the Officer arrived. He stood there watching me through the mirror and when I had completed my 'dummy' shave he curtly said, "Right Airman, that's fine now - join the others."

He then pointed out to the other lads that I was now a 'Properly shaven Airman.'

Disciplining a youth is one thing - but skinning him alive!!

Roll on demob!

Fleetwood, one evening during 'Bull Night', (the weekly 'spring clean' when the billet had to be cleaned from top to bottom ready for the next days inspection), got into a quarrel with a couple of the lads down at the bottom end of the room. I can't remember what it was about, but I fancy one of the lads had foolishly made some comment about Fleetwood's young lady. At any rate three or four of them ganged up on him (in the event not half enough), and the mighty miner, in a jiff, tipped up one of the beds and, (now empty of blankets) threw it at them pinning them to the wall. Before he could use that mighty hammer of a fist (and I knew just what it could do having seen our poor bedraggled 'Snowdrop' drop), I yelled, "Leave it - don't hit them," and he instantly stopped and turned to me.

"Good lad Fleetwood - they were only joshing - come on lets finish what we're doing and go down the NAAFI for an ale."

When we got back, the billet was in order and the whole incident was forgotten.

Fleetwood must have taken to me for, although we didn't correspond at all (poor chap could barely write anyway), I must have given him my address before he left Hednesford, because some time later I had a touching letter from him asking me to be his best man, as he was going to marry his lady love. Sadly, I had to decline, for what reason I can't remember, but I hope they had a very happy life together. For certain, no woman could have a man more in love with her than Fleetwood's young lady.

GETTING FIT

Each day we spent at least an hour at the gym where the PTI's (Physical Training Instructors) put us through gruelling workouts. These fellows had numerous ways of sorting you out, although in this instance I got on well with them, and in truth enjoyed every minute of what they gave us to do.

From PT, to cross-country running (I was good at that) day by day they got us all into shape. Of course this helped us with our drill, which continued to improve.

Until you go into the mob you don't realise just how much there is to marching. Learning to march (together) at different speeds. How to do the slow march (for funerals and the like). How to march with your rifle at the slope or carried low. How to mark time and how to wheel. How to fix bayonets whilst in a group without knifing the man next to you. (or cutting your own finger off for that matter) How to salute with and without your rifle.

How to halt - together!

How to come to attention - how to stand at ease.

I can't say it was fun (unlike the PT) but you certainly had to concentrate when on the parade ground, and Corporal Watson was the man 'to make a man of you.' He favoured no man, and was positively cruel to others.

Day by day we started to come into shape. And I have to say, it was most satisfying to be marching in unison with 120 men, heads held high and the crunch - crunch - crunch of our boots all hitting the shale of the parade ground all at the same time.

The second week saw the pace stepped up, and although they worked us hard, I noticed the NAAFI breaks (tea and a bacon wad) were getting a little longer to enable us recover. We were introduced to the Tommy gun and to the Bren-gun, and the armaments Sergeant showed us how to dismantle them, clean them and put them back together. We were shown how to load the differing magazines for the various weapons with the 303 calibre bullets they all used. It was particularly pointed out how important loading these magazines were as the weapon obviously would be useless if it jammed.

We were shown how to clean and look after our Lee Enfield rifle, and how to keep our rifle dry and oiled and how to keep our bayonet sharp. It was now that we began to realise that this was no game and that we were in it for real.

It was at the end of this second week of gruelling marching that my old ankle started to play up a bit. The old boy could take most of what life had to offer, but usually, after a hard game of football on a muddy pitch, or bowling fifteen overs at cricket, it needed a day off to recover. Although it permanently ached, I knew that with a little bit of rest it would soon be back to 'normal'.

I found that what with the heavy boots and the incessant marching and stamping, I was going to struggle. Apart from Sundays, my ankle had no time to recover. Of course I did not know how long this regime would continue and so I 'went sick' and reported to the M.O.

When he saw my ankle he nearly had a fit.

"What ever have you done Airman" he exclaimed.

And when I told him the story of my old swinger he (after examining my records at some length) said,

"Well Airman you are not fit to continue your service, we shall have to see about invaliding you out"

"Please don't do that sir," I pleaded. "I will be alright I promise you. I just need a little bit of rest occasionally to put it right."

"O.K. but it's excused boots for you for three days."

I was given an 'excused duties' note and told to report daily to the Gymnasium for sensible exercises. I was given a 'chitty' to give to the PTI.

The first morning at the Gym there was another Irkie there from another part of the camp. Although I was there with a legitimate problem, he was 'swinging the lead'. The PTI told us what exercises we had to do (although I knew exactly what I had to do to 'cure' my problem), and he left us to get on with it. My old ankle needed to have the weight taken off of it, and gentle rotating motions first one way and then the other. So I sat down and lit up a 'fag', soon to be joined by my skiving mate.

The second morning on arriving at the Gym we found a note from the PTI simply saying 'Same as yesterday - no slacking.'

We took him at his word and sat down and lit up.

Chattering away and using the occasional bit of 'Dockers language', we laughed and swapped tales from home. He was a lad from Cumbria, and his dad was a shepherd and (so he said) the current fell running champion. He told me that they had three black and white Border Collies, and that he missed them more than his mum's cooking.

Suddenly, after about twenty minutes or so of chatter, from behind a couple of stacked exercise benches, there slowly rose the most beautiful pair of legs you could wish to see.

"Bloody hell" my companion whispered "There's a girl in here."

The legs stretched ceiling-ward with the ankles twisting and turning very slowly, not unlike the movement of a belly dancer's hands.

We sat mesmerised. Eventually I called,

"Hello! Who's there?" and the legs slowly descended and disappeared from whence they came. Moments later a blonde curly head appeared followed by a slender, pretty boy, clad in a PT vest and shorts.

"Do carry on chatting - I was most intrigued by your stories," he said.

It turned out that he was a recruit as were we, but even as a naïve eighteen year old, I could see he wasn't quite the same as us. He had a narrow waist and not the semblance of a beard. But what twigged it for me were his long blond eyelashes.

"They sent me down here to build up my leg muscles as I really do struggle with the marching up and down. And doesn't that Corporal shout a lot. Sometimes I feel I want to cry."

We never saw him again.

One thing for sure, I learnt at a very young age that we are all different, and God just might get things wrong sometimes.

It was about this time that we were all asked if we would volunteer to give blood, as the donation unit was due on camp. At that time, whilst I would have said I was pretty fearless of anything, I did have this fear about giving blood. It was more a paranoid fear of having a needle inserted into the inside of my arm. Thankfully I have long overcome that fear, but at that time I wasn't too keen to have a go, but all the lads willingly put their name down, and although I said nothing I could not refuse to join them for fear of being accused of cowardice.

We gathered outside the medical hut and we had to queue up on a set of wooden steps that led to the waiting pretty nurses. Chicken hearted, I lingered at the back of the queue, all the while feeling more and more nauseous. Eventually, with just a dozen or so left, I had no option but to join the queue, and determined not to be last, nipped in four or five from the end. I had just reached the top of the steps and the door, when the M.O. came out and said,

"Thank you lads but we have got enough for today, we will take the rest of you next week."

What relief. Unbelievably they never came back, and I never got to expel my demons.

One day I decided to visit the camp dentist as small piece of filling had come out of a tooth. Although in no discomfort I thought it wise to do so as I was unsure when my next visit to my own dentist would be.

Sitting down in this young Dental Officer's chair (he was barely older than me) he appeared to ignore what I said was the problem, and after giving the inside of my mouth a cursory glance, tut – tutted to himself and muttering,

"I have never seen such a filthy mouth before in my whole career," (whole career? – it must have been all of a fortnight by the age of him) before putting some foul tasting liquid into my mouth which instantly turned into a dark foam and which I spat out into his waiting bowl.

"I'm going to have to take all your teeth out Airman – or you are going to be very ill."

"I don't think so sir," I said getting out of his chair, "There's nothing wrong with my teeth, I visit my dentist regularly."

"Sit down Airman – that's an order" the boy Dracula barked. "Good morning sir" I said, and hurriedly left his den of canine extraction, leaving junior to practice on someone else.

Luckily my 48 hour leave was due soon after and I arranged to see my own dentist – a Mr. Vernon Scard - who practiced from my two maiden aunt's house, and he kindly came to his surgery on the Sunday morning to see me.

"There is absolutely nothing wrong with your teeth," he said once he had replaced the lost filling, and he gave me a letter to that effect to take back to camp.

Fortunately it was not needed, as I heard no more from Dracula and his barbarism.

We Learn How To Kill

Bayonet practice was to some a laugh, but to others a great fear.

Three fairly realistic dummies were suspended on frames some 30 yards away from us as we all lined up in threes. At the command "Squad to Fix Bayonets - Bayonets - FIX", the metallic click, as our lethal bayonets locked into place, sent the adrenalin flowing.

The first three would attach their bayonets before the order "CHARGE" was given, whereupon you ran screaming at the top of your voice and plunged your bayonet into the unfortunate dummy. In one movement you withdrew your bayonet and brought the butt of your rifle up smashing the now unhappy dummy under the chin. Then, stepping to one side, the assailant ran a further 10 yards, still screaming loudly, before thrusting said bayonet into a prostrate second dummy before stepping on its neck and withdrawing the weapon.

Many times we had to do this exercise, and each time we did it you realised that they were turning us into a killing machine. The weaker men amongst us, who found the whole ordeal distasteful, were scoffed at and berated by the NCOs, and were forced to keep going until they showed enough venom in their actions. It was a strange, unique experience, both frightening and somehow exhilarating at the same time.

During the third week of our training, the weapons instructors decided that having been taught to clean and dismantle the weapons, we were ready to learn how to fire them for real.

We were to use live ammunition on the firing range.

When we saw the damage these things could do, we knew that we were not playing Cowboys and Indians.

Firing the Bren-gun was a joy. It was fired from the prone position with the barrel firmly supported on its two legs. It had very little recoil and you could use it as a single shot or as a machine gun. Either way it was extremely accurate. You were taught how to load your own magazines, and it was forcibly pointed out that if you did it improperly the gun would jam. In this event it was hells job correcting the error. You were reminded that in a battle situation, if this occurred, your incompetence would almost certainly cost both your own and your Comrade's life.

We all took care in learning to load those magazines, not wanting to be the fool whose gun jammed. My gun didn't jam, thankfully, but I blotted my copybook later nonetheless whilst on the range and using live ammunition.

The Lee Enfield rifle that every airman possessed (although they were always kept locked away in the armoury) was the soldier's friend.

Weighing in at about 9 ½ lb it was no light weight and it grew heavier as you marched around during drill throwing it from shoulder to trot and all points west. But as a weapon it was excellent - very accurate and very reliable. You were awarded a Marksman's badge (highly treasured) if you could put a clip of five bullets into a five-inch circle from 100 yards. You were also rewarded with a (I think) 2/- per week pay rise for achieving this. Try as I might I never achieved the coveted badge. I could regularly get four out of five in that target - but the whole five!

The rifle had quite a kickback when you fired it, and it was important that you kept it held tight to your shoulder or you could end up pretty sore.

When using live ammunition (always on the firing range) very strict safety measures were enforced, and to my shame I almost (or could have) caused a nasty accident. The Lee Enfield is a right-hander's weapon as the bolt action is located on the right hand side of the gun to enable a swift and easy ejection of the spent cartridge and the reloading of the next bullet. Although right handed I had great difficulty in keeping my left eye closed when aiming and was given permission to fire left handed. This meant that the bolt action was right in line with my left cheekbone and when (which was inevitable) I failed to ram down the bolt tightly on one occasion, it sprang back striking me a very nasty blow on the cheekbone. Idiotically I stood up still holding my rifle and with blood pouring down my face. It's a wonder there wasn't more blood as the instructor kicked the rifle out of my hand and threw me to the floor.

"Court Marshall for you laddie - doing that after all you have been taught. If that rifle had gone off you might have killed one of your mates."

How right he was - what an idiot.

Thankfully they let me off, but in punishment I was not allowed medical treatment until the session was over.

We were given theoretical training on how to survive in the wild.

They used as a guide the survival tin that all ditched airmen would be carrying when in battle conditions The tin contained about 9lb of goodies including a large bar of dark chocolate and high protein cubes of beef extract. There were also 10 cigarettes and a box of matches. What amazed me was that about 3lb of that tin was made up of curry powder. When I asked the Sergeant why this was so, he gave me a pitying look and said,

"Laddie, if you are out in the jungle and starving, you'll eat rotting dog, and if you mix curry powder with it, it makes it taste palatable."

I didn't like curry before this lesson, and I like it even less now.

In about the sixth week we were to put all this training to practical use. We were marched, weighed down with about 40lbs of equipment, for about ten miles or so, from the camp and up into the forest at Cannock Chase. Tents were erected - cooking facilities prepared - water fetched from the stream and put on to boil, and operational orders issued. Half a dozen of the lads were picked at random to act as cooks, whilst another eighteen were to act as camp guards. The rest of us were split into two groups and were to be given other tasks to perform. For my part (surprisingly as old Watson didn't like me) I was put in charge of 50% of the remaining lads, and we were to compete with the other group in various initiative tests set over the next couple of days. I was also told that my section's main job was to defend the camp over the next two nights from the 'enemy' made up from the rival group.

They were told that they had to take our position 'at all costs.'

It wasn't exactly a war, but the NCO's made it sound as though it was, and as Corporal Watson had assigned himself with the 'attackers', and I and my 'defenders' team was overseen by Corporal 'Baby Face' Rolfe, the sneers and threats between the two D.I.'s of whose team would come out on top, continued throughout the day.

During the day each team were to build a bridge over a shallow ravine and get our equipment across. At the same time we had to build a substantial shelter for our 'ammunition' to be stored in.

Both tasks were to be done in competition with the other team, and no help was forthcoming from the NCOs. I am pleased to say that 'Baby Face' kept right out of the way and left us to it. Apart from strutting around the building site with his swagger stick under his arm, and wearing a self-satisfied smile at our progress, he said little.

Our bridge was a beauty. Talk about the 'River Kwai' effort. You could almost have driven a train across it (well the Hornby variety at any rate). Luckily, I had a couple of young professional builders in my mob, and what with that, and the power of Fleetwood's muscle, I was able to quickly organise them into small groups that spread the workload, allowing them to get on with things and not get in one another's way. By 5pm we were finished and we were sat down having a fag. The opposition were a complete shambles.

The grub smelt good, and we were more than ready for it when it was dished up. We had heard a rumpus from the direction of the improvised cookhouse earlier on in the day, and at six o'clock (meal time) we found out what it was all about. Apparently the lads who had been seconded as cooks had used up three days rations on the one meal…Brilliant!

"Enjoy that nosh lads cos these brilliant boys have used up three days rations concocting this gourmet delight. There's no more left. For the next two days you will be living on porridge and bread and water," said a gleeful Sergeant Moore.

It was no joke, they had too, and it looked like we were going to have to live on porridge and scrambled egg for the next two days.

No one moaned as we all realised that it could easily have been one of us in the cookhouse, and I bet the NCOs didn't give them any guidance and simply let them ruin the food.

All was not completely lost, for, the next morning a large bundle was found in the cookhouse tent containing four or five rabbits, a couple of plump baby woodpigeon, three or four chicken and a couple of dozen eggs. There was even a Hedgehog. All provided (as we found out later) by Gypsy Joe, who had sneaked off of his defensive position during the evening and put his real talents to work. It was barely enough for 120 men but it certainly helped eke out what our fledgling cooks had left us.

The NCOs must have known who the benefactor was, but nothing was said and no medals handed out.

The second morning a similar, if smaller bundle was found.

As I was in charge of the defence of the perimeter of our encampment for the next two nights, I gathered my lads together to brief them on my strategy.

We were encamped in what appeared to be a large circular emplacement which had a quite steep earthen embankment around it. It had probably been an old Roman fort 2000 years before. This embankment was mostly quite steep and probably twenty feet or so in height in places.

The rules of engagement were handed out and included the command - 'Spotted - Killed,' if you shone your torch on someone. The 'spotted' fellow had to come forward and have a 'dead' sticker stuck on his back and a big letter 'D' written on the back of his hand in indelible ink. If the 'enemy' refused to acknowledge his 'spotted' shout you were allowed to get physical.

Having had a sneaky 'shufty' at the terrain in daylight, I deployed my men around the circle but in a zig-zag conformation so that each covered the other. I deliberately kept what I judged to be a 'tough going' section with masses of prickly gorse to overcome, very thinly patrolled and took a large chunk of that section myself. My second in command would use his whistle to warn me of the major attack, which of course we knew was bound to come.

All was quiet until about 2am when I heard a twig snap in amongst the gorse, and I could see a shadowy figure break cover and start to scramble up the very sleep slope directly below me. I let him get near the top then shone my torch right in his eyes saying "Spotted - Killed."

It was Corporal Watson. The fool kept coming on, ignoring a second 'spotted' call.

"Looking for a V.C. eh Corp." I said "Posthumous I'm afraid," as I punched him hard on the nose as he thrust his head over the top of the bank. With not a sound he disappeared into the blackness from whence he came, rolling down the steep bank and into the prickly gorse.

We repelled all boarders that night, 'Killing' most but taking a few prisoners.

Naturally I was pleased with myself when, in the morning, I was called to the Squadron Leader's tent to be congratulated, as I thought, for my brilliance as a defending commander, only to be confronted by a sorry looking, but furious, Corporal Watson, and an equally miffed Officer.

"Explain yourself Airman?" the officer said.

Which I did.

I was sent outside, and after ten minutes or so called back in to be told that I had been put on a 252 (charge sheet) and I was to report for sentence when we were back at camp. When I did report, I was given 5 days 'jankers' - and for what? Just obeying orders!

On the third day we packed up our kit and lined up for the ten-mile march home.

We were marching back to camp tired, dirty and hungry.

This journey, for me, was another learning curve. Dad had told me that on a march - if I could manage it - always to get in the front of the column. This day - forgetting dad's advice - I was at the back. The front of the column marched briskly, whilst us poor souls at the rear, seemed to be always running to catch up When we did manage it, the column would stretch out once more before concertinaing again like some gigantic caterpillar crawling along the forest tracks. I could see then why men marched to the beat of the drum, and how important it was for everyone to take the same size paces.

By the time we got back to camp I was exhausted.

Following a quick shower and change of clothes we were all hurried into the mess where the cooks (probably forewarned) did us proud with quite a feast. We all slept well that night, to be greeted the next morning with four hours marching practice.

This time we got it right.

THE FINISHING TOUCHES

We spent some time each week in the education block where we were taught RAF history and military law. The major lesson taught us was that you were wearing the Queen's uniform, and that at all times you must wear your hat and to be smartly dressed, as you were representing Her Majesty and your country. It was also explained that no Officer (commissioned or non - commissioned) was allowed to touch you, but at the same time you were obliged to always obey and order that either rank gave you. They could shout at you (and they often did) but they were definitely not allowed to touch you.

At meal times when the Duty Officer came around, you were entitled to complain about the food using the expression 'This meal is not fit for an Airman - Sir'. I only ever heard that complaint once, and sweet F.A. was done about it. Personally (and I was used to first class food at home) I rarely found much to moan about. It seemed to me that the cooks tried their best, and although it was pretty basic fare, there was always plenty of what was about.

Regarding the history of the RAF, I particularly remember the horror of seeing film of our lads coming home during the war, 'kites' shot to pieces, crash landing, being consumed in flames, and sometimes burnt to a cinder.

Most graphically of all, the sight of some poor rear gunner being (literally) hosed out of his turret into a body bag.

'PER ARDUA AD ASTRA' indeed.

These were brave lads for sure, and gave their all for us. Watching that film certainly quietened down some of the whingers for a while, and I can tell you, after watching those graphic scenes we all stood a little straighter on parade the next day.

After five weeks of hard discipline we were all granted a 48-hour leave. We were given a rail ticket home and told to report back by midnight on the Sunday. I can't remember anything about those two days off except mother's super Sunday roast, but I do remember a most pleasant incident on the train from Birmingham to Bristol.

I found myself sitting in a crowded compartment with all but myself and a very pretty young lady, absorbed in reading either their books or their newspapers. The young lady kept casting a shy but enticing smile in my direction and eventually she said,

"Are you a Pilot?"

"Oh no" I replied, "Just a simple Erkie."

"What's an Erkie?" She said, giggling coquettishly.

"Well it's not quite as good as a pilot, but you never know they might let me be one one day" I grinned.

The ice was broken, and we chatted away for some time before my pretty companion, who said that she was studying at Birmingham University and was on her way home to Cornwall for the summer break, asked if I would like to buy her a cup of tea in the restaurant car. Now this was 1956, and young ladies of the day were just not so precocious as they are today, and so I was quite taken aback by her invitation. But she WAS very pretty and there was a long journey ahead, and so I agreed.

Suffice to say we never made the restaurant car, for as soon as we were at the carriage join she stopped and boldly asked me to kiss her, 'as she had never before been kissed by a handsome young man in a uniform.'

That journey whizzed by, and to this day I never found out her name, and she certainly did not ask me mine. Yet a very intimate bond was forged on that train on our journey to Bristol.

When I alighted at Temple Meads, with a brief wave from the open carriage window, and an enticing smile she was gone forever.

On the Sunday evening dad drove Derek Wheeler (a local village lad, who was also stationed at Hednesford) and me over to Mangotsfield station (now defunct) to catch our train north to Birmingham, where we were to change for Hednesford.

When the train pulled in at Mangotsfield it was packed to the rafters. We managed to squeeze aboard and were crammed into the corridor with our bulging rucksacks at our feet. After five minutes of this playing at 'Sardines' I said to Derek,

"Come on mate follow me."

Squeezing our way through the crush of four or five carriages we suddenly arrived at the first class section, and lo and behold - no crush and two empty seats in the very first compartment. In we got, threw our rucksacks on the rack, and settled down to a few 'tut-tuts' and black looks from our travelling companions. I smiled benignly at everyone and wished them a good evening and whipped out a packet of Players. Before I could even open the packet, I was authoritively informed by a grim looking lady sitting in the corner,

"This is a no-smoking compartment young man. Can't you read?" She said pointing at the sign stuck to the window.

So it was.

"I'm sorry" I said, "I do like to stick to the rules, I will refrain."

Within twenty minutes or so, the call of "Tickets please" could be heard down the carriage.

"We will see who obeys rules now young man" said the very snooty grim lady triumphantly. The lady, who was wearing much too much jewellery to be elegant, sniffed loudly as she frumped herself up in an attempt to show importance.

Wheeler rose to take his rucksack down from the rack.

"Sit down Derek - all is not lost," I said smiling.

Before the ticket collector had even pulled back the door a triumphant gleam came into his eye as he spotted our uniforms.

"Tickets please" he said proffering his grubby hand into which I placed my off-green pass to Birmingham.

"This is a third class ticket and you are in a first class compartment."

"Indeed it is, and indeed I am" I said.

"Then you either get out and go back where you belong, or fork out the extra money," he said aggressively.

"Excuse me" I said "Who do you work for?"

"British Rail - who do you think?" he spat irritably.

"And who do you think I work for" I said pointing at my RAF badge.

Noting his confusion I explained politely.

"I work for Her Majesty Queen Elizabeth, through her government, the same as you do. Therefore, as I am travelling on company's time, on company's business, and on company's transport, I would imagine it should be at company's expense - don't you think?"

Flabbergasted - confused and completely bewildered our ticket collector spluttered,

"Right then - but if a first class passenger gets on at Gloucester and wants a seat, you will have to give over" and he slammed the door behind him.

"You're amazing Rog." said Derek "You even had me convinced."

"Thank you son" said the gentleman opposite, "He didn't ask for my ticket and I'm third class too."

Tossing a packet of Capstan Full Strength across the compartment he smiled and said,

"Keep the packet my boy and have a smoke on me when you get to Birmingham."

During our eight weeks training we were allowed one 48-hour pass (as explained) to go home (with rail ticket provided) and two passes to leave camp and go to Cannock the nearby town. A camp bus was provided to take us to town and bring us back. I only went to town once and can remember nothing of it, or of the town for that matter, save for an amusing incident that occurred as we sat on the bus waiting to be taken back to camp.

Standing on the pavement near the front of the bus appeared a man and a woman of about forty years of age who were arguing for all they were worth. The shouting got louder and louder, and when the lady began screaming abuse the man suddenly lost his patience and cuffed her around the ear sending her to the ground. One of the lads at the front of the bus leapt out to confront the man, only to be berated about the head with a brolly by the stricken lady who yelled.

"Don't you attack my husband you oaf," before walking off with her man, arm in arm.

You couldn't make it up.

BACK FLIGHTED

Eventually, that unfit, ill disciplined rabble that had come through Hednesford camp gates some eight weeks before, having learned to march, to fire guns, and how to kill with a bayonet, looked something like a disciplined fighting unit.

Further more, when we were on parade we not only looked smart and disciplined, we were very pleased and proud of ourselves.

Sergeant Moore and his D.I.'s had made men out of us in eight weeks indeed.

All that drilling and marching was to culminate in a big passing out parade. At the last minute I was summoned to the Squadron Leader's office and informed that I would not be taking part in the passing out parade, as I had been 'Back Flighted' for being undisciplined. I couldn't believe it.

I thought that I had been one of the best recruits in our flight at pretty much everything we did, and even imagined I might get the best recruit award.

Back flighted! I was sickened.

Perhaps my 'silent insubordination' on occasion had registered. Whatever the reason, the RAF had the last word, for, as the lads drew wads of pay and set off home for 15 days leave, I was left alone in my billet with the prospect of fourteen days extra square bashing.

I said goodbye to all of my mates (probably for the last time) and it was a slightly chastened A.C. Plonk Northam as I made my way back to a now empty billet. I was to live here alone for the next two weeks as the flight I was to join were living on the other side of the vast camp.

I thought that I had better check out that this was to still be my accommodation, and so plodded through the empty billet next door to mine where Corporal Watson lived in the NCO's quarters. Tapping on the door I was greeted with a cheery "Come in" followed by a momentary look of panic as Watson realised it was me. I said nothing but was glad that his conscience had caught up with him.

"What do you want?" he stammered.

"It's alright Corporal," I said "I haven't come to exact my revenge, I just need confirmation of my accommodation - that's all."

"You stay where you are until you finish your extra training" he said, slightly relieved that I wasn't going to address his unfair actions.

The one good thing about living alone was that I wasn't asked to 'bull' the billet, and so I had Tuesday evenings off. The bad news was that I had half a mile or more walk to join my new square bashing mates every morning.

That first day though, sitting on my bed in an empty billet that for the previous eight weeks had rang to the banter of a group of young men all experiencing a whole new life, was probably the worst moment of my whole two years in the RAF. But it was no good getting morose. Another day, another experience. A new bunch of mates, and a whole new world out there.

But at that moment in time I was a long way from home at RAF Hednesford in Staffordshire.

Hednesford one of the bleakest of the RAF's square bashing camps. Not the best place in the world to live alone.

My new Drill Instructor seemed a completely different type of person to Watson, and though firm and decisive, had got his men into marvellous shape. I was delighted when he immediately promoted me to point for the big passing out parade, and I felt privileged to receive the honour.

I cocked that up of course.

On the dress rehearsal the day before the big day, I was out on my own at point, with bayonet fixed and with rifle at the slope, when (as I thought) a fly landed on my right cheek and no matter how many times I tried to blow it off from pursed lips, the damn thing persisted in annoying me. I could not move a muscle of course as the slightest movement would have stood out like a sore thumb. Then to my great relief a Squadron Leader appeared on the square and I was ready to squash the little horror as I threw up a salute. What a fool I must have looked as the order came and I (having deftly got the fly - it turned out to be a globule of sweat perched irritatingly on those fluffy hairs just below the eye) threw up a salute only to realise in that instant that in these circumstances your salute is across the chest and rifle and not to the head. Although swiftly rectified, as I slid my hand from head to chest, I was of course spotted, and the D.I. was across the square in a flash.

With his eyes popping out of his cheeks, and he now angrily screaming abuse in a stream of coarse invective at his idiot point, as he stood but inches away from my face, I truly thought that he was about to have a heart attack.

He was so unhappy that he had been so stupidly let down, and he eventually shouted,

"Get off my parade - at the double - off this square you plonker. You are a disgrace to me and to the RAF.

Get back to that tosser Watson. I never want to see you again."

Shamefully I doubled off the square and out of that Corporal's life.

I never did get to pass out - and I got no passing out leave - just an order to report to Pool Flight straight away.

Back-flighted and now shamefaced to Pool-flight.

What next lay in store?

POOL FLIGHT

As I made my way to the Pool Flight billets carrying my full kit and not a few regrets for not behaving like a disciplined Airman should, I knew that Father would have been disappointed with me.

Pool Flight consisted of just a couple of huts tucked away in the corner of the very large camp that RAF Hednesford was. The camp was used exclusively for square bashing, and consisted of eight flights that turned out one fully trained batch of 120 young men every week. Each Flight was housed in six huts and the huts were dispersed around the enormous square that was situated in the centre of the camp. The Guardroom was just inside the main entrance, whilst the Gymnasium and Mess along with the administrative blocks were strategically placed between the billets, along with the very large NAAFI.

The two huts that housed Pool Flight, whilst I was there, rarely held more than a dozen men, as the lads were constantly coming and going.

Pool Flight was simply a place to put men who for the time being were 'homeless' and awaiting a posting.

Putting my kit bag on a vacant bed I was greeted by a cheery, chubby, freckle cheeked lad who wore spectacles.

"Welcome to paradise" he chortled.

"I've been here six weeks. I reckon they've forgotten all about me."

"What makes you say this is paradise?" I asked after introducing myself.

Howard Feddy was this lads name and although only my age (just eighteen) he definitely seemed more worldly wise than me.

"No work here Rog. - just eat, sleep and laze around. And it's a goldmine too."

He told me that he came from Leeds, and when asked what he did for a living in Civvy Street, he laughed and said that he was a Mock Auctioneer.

"What the hell is that?" someone asked.

He explained that he was part of a team that bought (mainly seconds) goods on the cheap and hawked them around the many markets in his area and selling them direct to the public off the back of a lorry. In the summer months, he said, they did a roaring trade at Blackpool with all the holidaymakers taking their annual break from the dreary drudge of the Lancashire cotton mills.

"Blimey" said one of the lads "That's dodgy - does it make any money?"

"About £100 a week" said Howard. "But don't tell the tax man."

And with that he produced a bulging wallet that looked as though it had his last months wages inside it.

Now remember, this was 1956, and a highly skilled man barely made £10 per week In fact, married men with whom I had worked in the chocolate factory just prior to joining up, were on £6:2:6d per week; so this chubby little fellow's bragging produced a mixture of shock and disbelief.

"How does it work?" asked one of the lads.

"Well, we usually work in fours. There's a 'Barker' who with loud humorous banter, draws in the crowd. Once assembled he hands over to the 'sweetener' who gives out little 'freebees' (combs - hairgrips and the like) to titivate the audience, before getting one of his 'Plants' in the audience to pay him 5/- for an unopened box to take a chance on what is in it.

"Who would like to gamble on what's in this box? It might be rubbish it could be something great?"

Eventually he 'sells' his box to his 'plant' and everyone, naturally, is eager to see what the man got for his 5/-.

His 'gamble' pays off, and the contents of said box is usually worth £5, and of course the 'lucky' purchaser is delighted, and shows it around to everyone there.

The 'sweetener' then sells as many 5/- boxes as he can. Usually he 'only has ten lucky chances!' and so there tends to be a scrabble to make sure they don't miss out. The 5/- 'gambles' are swiftly taken, but this time the punter is not given his box. These are left on the table in an enticing pile for all to see. The 'sweetener' then hands over to the 'salesman' who then proceeds to sell everything in sight at knock down prices all accompanied with a load of humorous banter that keeps the crowd entertained. China - Clocks – Stockings- Radios. All sorts of gear. He doesn't hand over the 5/- boxes until he has sold all his wares, and the people who bought them won't leave until they get their box, and so we are guaranteed a crowd – 'cos a crowd always draws a crowd.

Usually at Blackpool, we can get a cheeky Lancashire factory lass to climb up onto the back of the lorry and try on a pair of Nylon Stockings in exchange for five free pairs. The crowd love the spectacle, and of course the young lady enjoys her five minutes of fame.

Money for old rope - or in this case for laddered stockings."

"People won't swallow that guff," said a stolid looking lad from Norfolk.

"They do pal - with the right patter people will buy anything. I will show you. If each of you bring a couple of items from your kit bag and put them on this locker and I will demonstrate."

Full of curiosity by now, we all did as we were bid.

Howard then proceeded to launch into his patter.

I couldn't possibly do it justice, but within minutes he had us all in hysterics.

"You might think this gear is so cheap it's stolen. It's not stolen, it fell off the back of a lorry going up the Great North Road - he pushed it and I caught it."

Holding up a set of 'irons' (knife fork and spoon)

"This cutlery was made in Sheffield. That's Sheffield England not Sheffield Hong Kong where they sleep ten in a bed and keep Granny up the chimney."

Holding up a small padlock that we used to fasten our lockers with.

Banging it hard on the table he said

"Look at this lock - solid brass - you could use this to secure - The White House - a Lighthouse - Workhouse - Shhhh…..ed."

Mesmerised we gazed in awe as he, one after the other, sold the items in front of him.

"Never mind a pound - never mind ten bob. Don't even think of half-a-crown - one and nine or even a shilling. Who'll give me a tanner for this lovely bargain? Here you are sir it's yours. Don't tell anyone where you bought it or we'll all be killed in the rush."

To us poor rookies we were in the presence of genius.

Even Norfolk Ned bought his 'irons' back for a shilling.

The man was worth every penny of his £100 per week.

I liked Howard and he liked me.

"How are you off for cash Rog?" he asked me. "26/- a week doesn't go very far does it? If you don't mind getting dirty I can put you on to a small fortune."

I wasn't interested in a small fortune, but as we had nothing to do all day except to report to Admin. at 10am and 4pm to see if our postings had come through, I was game for anything, provided it was honest.

"Put your denims on, bring your kit bag (empty of course) and follow me," said my new Leeds chum.

All the wooden billets were built on stilts and stood a couple of feet off of the ground, and one by one Howard took me to them and got me to crawl underneath and retrieve the many flagon sized lemonade bottles that lay there.

"You've got to do the dirty work Rog. 'cos I'm the boss," he laughed.

We took the now full kit bags back to the ablutions and thoroughly washed the bottles, any damaged ones were discarded. The clean bottles were then taken to 'Smokie Joe's' the roadside café that stood permanently outside of the camp main gate. 'Smokie' sold bacon butties etc. and crucially his big seller was flagons of hot sweet tea for 2/6, which included 6d returnable on the bottle.

Howard had twigged that few Airmen would walk a mile or more (it was a big camp) to reclaim their 6d and disposed of their empties under the billet; and so had done a deal with 'Smokie Joe' to provide him with a good supply of clean bottles. Amazingly, sometimes we were making up to £5 per day between us.

A small fortune indeed!

"The big payday comes on Thursdays," said Howard "Every Thursday one flight are 'billet bound' bulling up their kit for the big passing our parade on the Friday. They have drawn their pay - plus their leave pay - and so of course are rich. We just go along and offer to go up to Smokie's for a wad and tea and they will be so grateful that they will all treat us to a drink or whatever."

Did I say the man was a genius?

As we went around the four billets taking orders, the tips piled up.

It got better, for Howard had done another deal with 'Smokie' and was getting a 10% discount on all orders. He even produced a small handcart that he had 'found' somewhere so that we could do our errands in just two journeys.

That first Thursday brought me in £22. Truly a goldmine.

"See Rog. You can make more money by using your head than ever you can by working."

On the first weekend of my Pool Flight days, I decided to hitchhike home.

I set out on the Saturday morning after an early breakfast, and as usual made good headway, sometimes only travelling a few miles and sometimes twenty miles or more, but always on the move south. All was going well until I found myself on the A38 at Worcester on a long fast stretch (not good for getting cars to stop) and had had no luck for an hour or more.

I had eaten my last piece of chocolate and was about to light up a 'Lucifer' when a smart looking modern car slowed rapidly and stopped some 100 yards ahead. I ran hard, and as I reached it the back door opened and I was greeted with a cloud of confetti and a cheery, "Hop in."

There in the front was a very happy, pretty bride with her equally happy and handsome new husband.

"Oh thank you" I said "But you have obviously just got married and I just could not intrude."

"Don't be silly," said the bride, "You will be our first good deed together in our married life, and you will bring us both good luck. We are going to Cornwall, where are you heading?"

"That's marvellous," I said. "I am going to Bristol, so it's on your way."

That wonderful couple chattered away as we sped south, and they asked me all about my service life to date.

In those days there were no motorways of course, and there wasn't too much traffic on the road either. After a while we caught up with and followed for some miles, another vehicle that had a very pretty young thing in the back who, when she saw us began excitedly waving, smiling and pointing, before finally making great play of writing something on a piece of paper and indicating that she wanted us to read it. She eventually threw it from the car and my driver stopped and retrieved it. Mysteriously the message read:

'Who is the handsome Airman in the back? Dad was behind you when you picked him up. My name is Pat McDonagh and I live in Chard."

And she had written her address.

Of course the car carrying the pretty writer of the note had now long disappeared, and the excited bride handed it to me saying,

"Now if I were you I would write to her when you have time. Isn't it romantic?"

I did write and we corresponded for a short while, although we never met, before I was lucky enough to meet Parvin soon afterwards and that was the end of that.

My lovely honeymoon couple dropped me off at Filton church and sped off to (I sincerely hope) a very happy life together. I had to 'hoof it' the last few miles as none of my fellow Bristolians were prepared to offer me a lift, but I didn't mind. Thanks to the kindness of my honeymooners I was still home a couple of hours ahead of schedule.

All too soon my posting came and I bade Howard and his Goldmine goodbye.

I was sent to RAF Compton Bassett in Wiltshire to be trained as a Wireless Operator (so much for my I.Q. of 154) and Howard - still forgotten- stayed at Hednesford. I wonder if he ever got away and if he did - how did 'Smokie Joe' manage for his empties.

A LIFE CHANGING MOVE

Arriving home for only my second spot of leave in four months and a whole summer's cricket wasted. I was looking forward to a couple of day's civilian life before starting my trade training. Not one game of cricket had I played that summer, and I was definitely getting withdrawal symptoms. Eighteen years of age and the time when most youngsters are honing their bowling and batting skills, and what am I doing? I'm marching up and down a barrack square honing my marching skills. As I have always said, when talking about cricket.

'If I'd practised, I would have played for England.'

But duty called, and although I had no choice - I went.

I spent my generous three days leave with my family before heading for Compton Bassett in Wiltshire to be instructed in the mysteries of the Morse Code and communication over the airwaves.

No prospect of flying for this Airman, simply hours of listening to dah-dit-dah and trying to make some sense of it.

I was placed in W.O.P. 30 with 20 or so other Erkies - and the drudgery began.

Four months of purgatory.

Although a very important job no doubt, I could tell within days this wasn't the job I was designed for. You needed no brains. You were not required to think. In fact you could have trained a chimpanzee to do it in a week.

Having said all of that, I somehow managed to fail the course.

One good thing came out of that posting, for it was at Compton Bassett that I met my good old mate Fred Nurk, and we shared a large chunk of our national service together.

Despite the drudgery of trying to get the hang of Morse Code, I also had great fun whilst at Compton. I met loads of interesting new people, and gained much great experience on the entertainments side, taking part in shows and learning how to stage-manage.

I played quite a bit of football for the camp team on a Wednesday, and was able to get home fairly easily on a weekend to play football for Hambrook, (almost exclusively for the Reserves).

Whilst at Compton Bassett though, my life changed forever.

Weekend leave was now regularly available, and I was soon back home to enjoy a bit of civilian life and of course mother's cooking.

I would normally hitchhike home on a Saturday morning. This was a fairly easy exercise in those days as people were very generous to young men in uniform and very often I could be home in an hour.

The lads in the village were keen to hear my story, as a lot of them had managed to worm their way out of doing their bit, and those that did were mainly in the Army. My brother Colin and Neil Ware were doing their service at the same time as I was - both in the RAF. Neil - a carpenter by trade - had been posted to a tiny island above the Shetlands called 'Hardrock'. He had been sent there to build an early warning Radar station. It was in the days of the cold war and as a nation we were fearful of the 'Ruskies' coming to get us. Brother Colin was in his last few weeks of training as a Radar Technician just a few miles further up the road from me at RAF Yatesbury. When he qualified he was given a real 'Jammy' posting to RAF Colerne barely a dozen miles from home. He, being a clever fellow, and although an Analytical Chemist by profession, had been made a Corporal Technician (they wore their stripes upside down) and was working on Radar.

Colerne at that time was an operational camp and flew all types of aircraft from it.

Eager to bring me up to date with the local news, the lads told me of the new intake of trainee nurses at Frenchay Hospital, and that amongst them was 'a beautiful Indian girl.' That evening we trooped down to Frenchay and standing in a bunch outside of Frenchay House (which was where the young trainee nurses were billeted) we requested to see the pretty young lady.

Soon a very shy young girl of indeed exceptional beauty was brought out to meet us. She spoke no English, for she was a beautiful Persian girl, not Indian at all, and I was instantly taken by her. When she made it known that she would like a cigarette lighter to observe us all individually in the fading light, my heart sank when she appeared to ignore me as she studied the other lads, seemingly, with care. She finally got to me and gazed up at me with those bewitching dark brown eyes. I just fancy she lingered a moment longer than she had with my friends, with the flickering flame between her face and mine.

"What is your name?" I asked smiling.

"Parvin" she replied, "What is yours?"

And so it was that I met the girl that was to be my wife and bear me three children. The first of which, a beautiful daughter called Zeba, sadly died three days after her birth of a congenital heart, before she bore me my handsome son Kion and equally beautiful daughter Laili.

Luckily for me the beautiful young nurse liked me and agreed to be my Beau, and so I now had an added incentive to get home on a weekend.

I did manage to make it most of the time. I was able to see my Persian Princess and snatch a game of football for my village at the same time.

When mother found out that I had settled down with 'a proper girlfriend' she was delighted. When I told her that she was a Muslim however, mother was aghast.

"Oh son, you're not going to marry a heathen are you?" she said.

"Why no mother" I said, "I'm going to marry a Persian - if she'll have me."

DAH-DIT-DAH-DAH

WOP 30 at Compton Bassett consisted of a very mixed bunch of lads from all over the U.K. and from all walks of life.

The lad who slept in the bed on my left hand was a Glaswegian called Miller. 'Jock', as he was fondly known, was only about 5ft 8ins tall and of wiry build. Sporting dark curly hair he was a very handsome chap despite a vivid scar that curved down his left cheek from cheekbone to chin. That scar was the legacy of a Gorbals street fight he informed me. He told me many horrific stories of what life was like in his part of Glasgow, and how he had been privvy to two murders and numerous beatings amongst his neighbours. The most horrific tale concerned his best friend who, on opening his front door in their tenement, was confronted with a maniac, who simply buried a cleaver in his skull before spitting out,

"You won't be saying that again Jimmy," and then walking off.

He was a tough cookie was Jock, but (luckily) he took to me and, as he had signed on for a three year stint and was paid considerably more than us national service lads, (we were paid the princely sum of 26/- a week), he would generously, and without fail, leave two woodbines on my pillow every Tuesday evening, knowing I would be broke as it was the day before payday.

Pay day – known as, 'The day the Golden Eagle shits.'

I had never asked Jock for a 'ciggie', or anyone else for that matter, and when at first I asked if it was he who had put them there, he simply growled in his thick Glaswegian accent,

"A man needs a smoke - so you smoke with Jock."

When I attempted to repay him, he would just glower at me, with his smouldering blue eyes boring into mine and say, "What ciggies?" and turn away.

Jock used to drink a lot, and always the day after payday he would leave the camp and go down to the nearest town of Calne and 'take a drop or two,' as he would put it.

Invariably he would return late at night - goodness knows how he got past the guards, as we all had to be back at camp by 11pm if we ever ventured out. We would all be tucked up in bed and fast asleep until the door was flung open and Jock would be standing there. He would stand, framed by the door for a few seconds, before shouting at the top of his voice, 'Guardiloo' and waking the whole billet, before staggering to his 'pit', and flopping on it.

He would be sending up the zz's within seconds of so doing, whilst the rest of us tried to get back to sleep. Nobody complained, it would have done little good as Jock would have almost certainly challenged the complainant, and probably treated him to a 'Glaswegian kiss' before settling the matter.

When quizzed, in his sober moments, on the meaning of his infuriating yell of 'Guardiloo', the smiling Jock explained that in Glasgow where he came from - when the occupants of the Gorbals tenements (that did not possess a personal lavatory) awoke, instead of taking their brimming chamber pots to the communal toilets, they would empty them out of the window, following the warning cry of 'Guardiloo.'

It was not wise to tread those streets at that hour without a brolly.

Jock loved his boxing as did I, and when the RAF team came to the camp to take on the Navy in the vast Gymnasium, he and I had a ringside seat. One of the sailors was known to Jock, and after he had proceeded to totally outbox our RAF lad for three rounds, Jock grabbed my arm and we made our way to the dressing room. There stood our victor, and Jock introduced me. To my complete amazement before me stood a brave young man sporting swollen lips - a reddened nose plus two ruddy ears, and a puff under his right eye seemingly swelling as we spoke.

"Pleased to meet you" I said, "Congratulations. But he didn't appear to have laid a glove on you" And pointing at his eye I said, "How come the mouse? You were all over him."

"Och aye" he grinned, "But don't go and have a look at him."

Jock Miller didn't box himself - he was street fighter. On one occasion it showed. Every Tuesday evening we had to 'bull up' the billet for the next days inspection This weekly ritual would take the whole evening and became quite a bonding exercise, as it was essential that the inspecting Officer and his NCO's found everything in pristine order, or we were all for the high jump. Amongst everything else, it was the linoleum-covered floor that had to be polished (nay, burnished) till it shone like glass. Once cleaned it was treated with positive reverence and we all skated across it on our own pads of towelling we wore instead of shoes. Heaven help anyone who broke this rule, as that blasted floor was treated like a delicate piece of porcelain. For the rest of the week one could walk on it normally of course, but even then you were careful not to skid about on it when wearing boots.

The evening chore was lightened by the playing of the popular songs of the day over the camp Tannoy system. The camp Tannoy boasted its own D.J. and requests would be aired from time to time. We mutually agreed that should one of our favourites be played the chatter would stop for the couple of minutes it was on. Now Jock was a great Sinatra fan and this particular evening, as 'Old Blue Eyes' came on to sing for our young Scottish Blue Eyes, a rather rowdy Londoner, who slept immediately opposite Jock, started shouting that Sinatra was old hat and Jock should get up to date with Bill Haley.

"Quiet" said Jock, "Or I will quieten you."

The foolish lad ignored the request, although to be fair he was only joshing, and Jock not wanting to miss any more of 'I've Got You Under My Skin,' stepped forward and with a neat clip of his right fist, knocked out our crafty cockney as sweet as a nut. The lad collapsed on to his bed, face down, and the music played on. As Mr. Sinatra finished his number our London friend began to stir and sat up groggily.

"I did ask," said Jock "That's my favourite song - so in future you might remember 'I've got you under my chin' and keep quiet."

Our cockney friend never did that again.

One evening a lorry load of us young Erkies were shipped up to Marlborough to a large old house that was being used as the billet for a group of student nurses, as they were holding a party.

The girls were pleased to see us and we all had a good time, none more so than the handsome Jock, who, as usual, had a little too much to drink, and as the alcohol took effect, proceeded to entertain us with a medley of songs that his cousin used as a Busker on the streets of Glasgow. He had quite a good singing voice, but all the songs were ruined by his infuriating habit of adding at the end of each line the word 'Ahhriddy.' Sometimes if the mood took him, he would even start a line with 'Ahhriddy.' The girls loved it though, and showered him with hugs and kisses at every opportunity.

I am glad that I met Mr. Miller. I often think of him and wonder how his life panned out. He was intelligent, but totally uneducated. I swear that if he had been born a doctor's son in the South of England, he would have gone to Oxford or Cambridge and become someone famous.

What a shame. I hope he had a good life.

It was whilst at Compton Bassett that the Suez crisis (war) took place.

We were all put on high alert, and a lot of the lads were taken to RAF Lyneham, (which was just down the road) to help load the Beverley transporters with ammunition and supplies. This I wasn't asked to do, but wished that I had been. It would have been nice to think I was doing my little bit for the lads. It was at this time too, that a dozen or so Irish lads on camp were whisked away. We found out later that they had been dismissed from the service as a precaution against trouble with the I.R.A. I must admit, the couple of Irish blokes I knew were top fellows, and one in particular was very disappointed that he could not continue with his RAF life.

Learning to be a Wireless Operator was not exactly rocket science, but could I get the hang of it? Could I hell.

I quickly learnt the Morse Code and how to send messages via the hand key. But I just could not receive. Well I could, but only when it was transmitted extremely slowly. In the classroom we all had our own Morse key and a set of ear phones, and we were able to tune in, so to speak, to any one or all of the class at any time, including the instructor of course. We were told to persevere and to particularly listen to our own transmissions. One day, it was explained, that instead of a series of dots and dashes we would hear, as if by magic, the message coming through as clear as a bell, not as dots and dashes but almost as though it was a voice speaking to us. The instructor assured us, the change would happen. It would be exactly like when you learn to ride a bike. Today you can't ride - tomorrow you can - and once you can ride a bike you wonder just how it was that you couldn't do it.

One by one my classmates shouted 'eureka,' until I was left there alone, struggling on about twenty words a minute, and that, all in dots and dashes.

No magic voice for me sadly.

We were given both practical and theoretical lessons on the actual Radio itself. I went along with all of this and, so the young Officer teaching us said, got on rather well with it. I confess that I have forgotten every word of those lessons, except for the time when I quizzed our instructor on how (as he told it to us) an electric current (signal) could travel along a wire in opposite directions at the same time. I remember that he waffled away for ages making less and less sense to me, before he irritably said,

81

"There is no need for you to know WHY - it just does."
Well I only asked!

So it was that at the end of the course all my mates passed their exam and were made up to LAC (Leading Aircraftsmen) and given with the promotion a £1 per week rise and a two-propeller badge for their sleeve. I was left as the class duffer and stayed an A.C. Plonk on 26/- per week.

I was pretty sick. It wasn't the money; it was just the fact that I had found something that I was proven useless at.

I was given a new title though - Telegraphist Assistant. (Tea boy)

My father once asked me "How come you're still an AC2?"

To which I replied, "Because there ain't no AC3's."

In fact it wasn't until I had been in the mob for eighteen months before I rose to the dizzy heights of AC1.

This remember, from a man with an I.Q. higher than Einstein!

THE OTHER SIDE OF COMPTON

My days at Compton Bassett enriched my young eighteen years in many ways. It was here for example that I witnessed two fifteen stone WAAFs sitting at the NAAFI bar smoking pipes and quaffing pints of brown ale. This was 1956 remember, and witnessing this was quite a shock to a young lad's system.

Amongst our mates in the billet was a fearless young man (whose name sadly escapes me) who had ridden in the Isle of Man T.T. and was the proud possessor of a 1000 cc Norton racer. It was an enormous machine. He used to ride it up from his home in Hampshire, and delighted in charging anyone who was brave enough, 10/- to, as he put it, join the 'ton-up club' on the back of his 'thunder bird.'

The main Calne to Yatesbury road that passed the camp had, fortuitously, a straight stretch the best part of a mile long just about where the narrow camp road joined it.

The 'ton-up' contenders would climb aboard the pillion and, hanging on for grim death, round the bend from the Calne end of the straight at 50 or 60 mph before, with a full throttled roar, flash past the spectators at over 100mph. Needless to say my 10/- stayed in my pocket as I had little wish to soil my trousers in front of the baying crowd. There were no helmets in those days and I had visions of cracking my skull, at the speed of light, against a Wiltshire wall.

No - not for me folks - I will stick to cricket.

I did, however, have a terrifying motorcycle experience during my Compton Bassett days. I used to hitchhike home on a Saturday morning so that I could play football for my village, and get to see my pretty young girlfriend. Most weeks it was no problem as people, as I have said, were very generous with lifts in those days to young men in uniform; but this day I had walked almost to Calne (two or three miles) with no luck before a motorbike pulled up.

"Jump on" the pilot yelled, "I'm going your way."

"I'm going to Bristol," I said.

"I know. I'm Sergeant Wilson from the cookhouse, and I had you drying plates for you're fatigues - remember?"

I did now - he certainly looked different in his pilots cap and goggles, and his leather jacket. He looked more like Biggles than Geoff Duke.

When I told him that I needed to be home in time for my game of football, he nodded and looked at his watch saying,

"Hold on tight - we will have to fly to make it."

Telling him about my football was a big mistake. Never mind the 'ton-up' club, I reckon there must have been moments on that hair-raising ride when we joined it. Having said that, we almost joined that mighty club in the sky on a couple of occasions, particularly when rounding a bend with shoulders (I swear) brushing the tar macadam. We firstly hit a large clump of mud and started to slide toward a high wall, before the intrepid Sergeant miraculously righted the machine, only to be confronted around the next corner by a herd of cows lazily going the same way as us and completely blocking our path. Disaster! But miraculously, some hidden hand parted that herd sufficiently at that precise moment to allow passage. (Just like the Red Sea was parted for Moses). But for that hand of Providence, my last sight on earth would have been disappearing up a cow's arse.

The flying Sergeant dropped me off at Kingswood High Street.

I was shaking like a leaf, grey as a medieval death mask, and too speechless to thank the man. But I was nearly home, and I was still in one piece (just), and good fortune was about to smile upon me once again that Saturday morning. This was in the shape of an immediate lift - only this time in the comfort of a Morris 8 driven by a kindly old gentleman who had, he said, done his little bit in the trenches in Flanders, and was pleased to be of assistance to someone who was prepared to fight for Queen and Country. He very kindly dropped me off outside The Star Inn at Pye Corner, and in the event in plenty of time for a cup of mother's tea and a cheese sandwich, before my game of football on the Common.

My good fortune held as I recall, as I had a fair game that day, scoring a couple of goals in a hard fought victory.

I have to confess that was the last time that I ever sat astride a motorbike.

I don't even get on them on a Carousel at a fairground.

A large part of the winter of 1956/57 was spent in the wooden billets at Compton Bassett, where the warmth was provided by two coke fired stoves set in the middle of the room. These stoves would glow in the dark after lights out, and from time to time, before we went to sleep, we would have a joke telling session. Each Erkie would take it in turns to tell their favourite gag or hilarious anecdote.

Much enjoyment was had during these sessions before we would mutually agree to tell one last joke each before sleep.

One such session produced (for me) the funniest joke - or at least the one that made me (by far) laugh the longest.

Having all, as agreed, told our last gag, we settled down to sleep, basked in the radiant red glow of the comforting heat of the stoves.

Some ten minutes had passed in complete silence when suddenly a lone voice piped up.

"Snow White and the Seven Dwarfs were in bed together, and they all wanted a little bit. She said NO - so they all got up Grumpy in the morning."

The wooden roof on our billet almost came off with the roar of laughter.

For me, I could not get back to sleep as I chuckled away all night long at this simple but hilariously funny joke. It still makes me laugh to this day.

I took part in the camp Variety Show during my Compton days, and although it was a great success it did not get off to a good start.

Turning up five minutes late for the audition, I was greeted by the camp Entertainments Officer. He was a young Pilot Officer with a cut glass accent and had a rather supercilious air about him. Ignoring my profuse apology and rather weak joke that I was expecting to see 'Palladium Hopefuls' written on the door, and not, as it was, 'NAAFI RUBBISH'; our budding Val Parnell said loudly, in an Etonian accent and sneering tone,

"There's always one 'tail-end Charlie' isn't there. Who might you be, the West Country's answer to Bing Crosby? More like Old Macdonald with that accent. HAW - HAW- HAW."

Stepping as close to the man as I dare without actually touching him, I hissed in anger.

"Just cos Iv'e got a country accent matey boy, don't think I haven't got a brain. I can out-think you mister in my sleep."

The Guardroom loomed but at that moment in time I cared not.

This ignorant little runt could get stuffed.

Visibly shaken, our young E.O. was speechless for a moment before he smiled weakly and said, "You must be an actor - or a comedian?"

"You are right Sir I am a comedian. Would you like to hear a joke?

"Oh yes please" our chastened officer replied, "Make us all laugh."

"Two leaves on a tree. One said to the other, hold tight I think I'm going to blow off."

The tension was broken as all that were there laughed, including the E.O. who clapped with boyish enthusiasm.

"You're in" he cried, "Come and meet the rest of the troupe."

The fellow turned out to be a good friend (if you can be friends with an officer) and listened to all my suggestions regarding the smooth running of the show when he learned that I had put on variety shows in my village before I joined up.

The show was a great success despite a couple of 'faux pas' - both of which were my doing. During my act I mentioned one of the pipe smoking WAAFs and her pretty friend called Rose.

'Rose I said was now known as the 'camp bicycle' - Every body rides it!!'

Although it got a big laugh, neither Rose nor her big friend, who were both in the audience, found it funny - which, on reflection, I suppose was probably right.

The other hiccup, in its way, could have been even worse.

I had persuaded the E.O. to include a number of one-minute sketches between acts, to help keep the show fast moving, and they were all successful with the exception of the old 'bucket of water' gag. This was where an awkward oaf carries a bucket of water across the stage a couple of times interrupting the artist at the mike. Each time he crosses the stage he stumbles and spills some of the water. Finally the chap on the mike says 'get rid of that water you idiot before you drown someone' and the oaf throws it at the audience. Of course the bucket has been switched for one filled with confetti, and the audience duck and dive before they realise it.

Very effective, and very funny.

The problem was, the bloke who put the confetti in the bucket didn't realise that there was two inches of dust and grime in the bottom and the Group Captain C.O., dressed in full regalia in the front row with his lovely wife, copped the lot. This got a big laugh too as you might imagine - but not from the C.O.

One of the acts in the show was a very talented Corporal who definitely could have made his living on the stage. He was multi-talented. He could sing, dance, tell jokes but for our show he was a hypnotist. Now up until this time I did not believe in Hypnosis, and thought it was all a fake. No longer do I believe this. For example he cured every one of the cast of smoking (unfortunately except me). But his act on stage was hilarious. He had men eating large raw onions and swearing they were eating peaches. He had people behaving like chickens and some behaving like parrots, but best of all he introduced a young Airman to a mop telling him it was Marilyn Monroe. He whispered to him that she had fallen in love with him, and would do his bidding. His amorous high jinks eventually had to be curtailed or he would have ended up with splinters of wood from the mop handle in a very delicate place.

As I say, the show was a great success, and a bonus came my way when the E.O. gave me and my good mate Fred Nurk the job of stage managing the ENSA shows that came to camp.

One such show was The Mick Mulligan Jazz Band, which included as their singer a young George Melly. George amazed me by sitting in the wings deeply immersed in large tome written by Tolstoy. Seemingly transfixed with his reading, he instantly came out of his trance the moment his name was called for his spot, when he would lay down his book, bounce onto the stage, and burst into song right on cue. One moment a very quiet studious young man, the next, effervescence personified. Song over, he would take his bow, pick up his book, and be immediately intently immersed once more until his next call. A real Pro.

When the show was over, Fred and I were invited to join the band in the NCO's club for a drink. Mick - a keen snooker player - asked if either of us could play as he wanted a partner to challenge the two 'stars' who were hogging the table on a 'winner stays on' basis. I could play of course, having been brought up with a quarter sized table at home, but Fred could really play. He joined Mick in what became a big game with a five-pound side stake, (an awful lot of money in those days) after Mr. Mulligan had (good naturedly) thrown down a challenge. The NCO had accepted the challenge but cleverly (so he thought) had made it a doubles match over five frames.

Fred was quite brilliant, producing a 72 clearance to rapturous applause, to win the first frame. Dear old Fred dominated the next two frames for a three nil victory and a crisp five pound prize for Mr. Mulligan.

Mick and he stayed at the table for the rest of the night, with Fred on another occasion producing another big clearance - this time of 96. What a pity it couldn't have been a 'ton.' However, he was the hero of the hour, and was rewarded, when the shutters eventually came down, with a couple of 'Blue Backs' (fivers), from the grateful and generous Mick. One of those prize fivers Fred kindly gave to me.

George Melly didn't play snooker, but I noticed that he finished his mighty tome before he went off to bed.

One of the outcomes of our successful camp variety show was that some 'outside' stage work was acquired (I can't remember how) and I performed in various localities in and around Calne including the rather splendid old Town Hall. My mate Fred could not be persuaded to step on stage with me and I had talked a rather shy chap who lived in my billet called 'Wally' Wareham (he was called 'wally' because he WAS a wally) into joining me as a stooge for various sketches on the stage. This shy puny lad, to be fair, began to enjoy being 'somebody' and became rather good at it, and he was more than grateful to pocket his share of the generous fees we were earning. So it was one hell of a shock when, on going up to him at his bed when our training course had ended, to shake his hand and wish him well, on hearing that he had drawn a posting to Christmas Island in the Pacific, for him to say,

"I don't want to shake your hand. I don't like you, and never have."

I thought he was joking, but he wasn't, and off he went to the Pacific leaving me a very puzzled man.

Fred Nurk acquired his unusual nickname when on introduction he shook my hand and said,

"I'm Bernard O'Donaghue from London known to all my friends as Fred Nurk."

"Then as I hope to be your friend - Fred Nurk you shall be," I said.

And so it was that 'Fred' was born.

Apart from snooker, Fred, who loved all sports, was pretty useless at performing. He told me he played the game (football – cricket - whatever) through watching, and that was why he particularly enjoyed having me as a mate. He never missed a game of football or cricket match that I played in, and even if I had a bad game he always had something upbeat to say. He would probably have made a great football manager. He was a Bookmakers Clerk by profession, and had an amazing gift with numbers. Fred taught me how to keep a book, the secret being continually adjusting the odds as each wager is taken to ensure that which ever horse won the 'book' always made a 10% profit. Amazingly, Fred could absorb all these ever changing figures, odds – wagers laid etc. in his head, and was able to instantly warn his 'governor' when to adjust his board. His party piece with the lads was equally amazing. During a game of darts, the instant the third dart hit the board he would immediately make up the score that was left with one, or a combination of, Bingo calls.

For example:- if 170 was required he would yell, seemingly without thinking,

"Two fat ladies, unlucky for some, and anyway round."

Which reads to the uninitiated: - 88+13+69, which of course equals 170.

He was never wrong, and when, on a quiet moment, I asked him how he did it, he said he didn't know - it just automatically happened in his head.

Smashing bloke Fred, and a good friend. Sadly he died in his early thirties of Rheumatoid Arthritis. I bet he's having fun helping Saint Peter keep his book. If so I look forward to offering you my number Fred, but not for a little while yet please.

One of Fred's great enjoyments was having a game of 'Housey - Housey' (now called Bingo), and every payday evening they would play it in the NAAFI. Personally I wasn't at all keen as I found it a most puerile game that I'd left behind with Snakes and Ladders. However, Fred enjoyed it, and so I would reluctantly be dragged along in the vain hope (as Fred would put it) 'to strike it lucky' and win the jackpot. In truth I only went along to please Fred, as he was such a loyal mate and did most of the things that I wanted to do without question. I used to pay my 6d for a card for each game, and Fred paid his 2/- and always had four.

I might have thought that 'Housey -Housey' was a puerile game, but it was very popular, and most weeks it was standing room only. What a waste of money I used to think, but then Fred didn't smoke as I did, and he always said that tanning your lungs was a waste of money, and he was probably right.

A lot of the lads would stay in the billet and play brag. I enjoyed a game of cards, but I preferred to go down to the NAAFI for a game of snooker. It was a joy to play snooker with Fred because he was so much better than me and walloped me every time. He tried to show me how to get better control of my cue ball, but I played snooker like I played golf (give the ball a bang). However, when the 'Housey-Housey' began, Fred always enticed me to put the cue down and join in his 'Jackpot' game.

Fred was adept at both pastimes, and whereas I struggled to keep up with - 'Seven and Six - was she worth it,' 'All the three's – Feathers,' 'Five and Nine the Brighton line' etc., Fred could play his cards four at a time comfortably.

One such night with my mind totally bewildered with 'Clickity-click' and 'Doctor's chum' (why they didn't just call out the numbers I will never know) and with Fred sat opposite me scratching away like a good 'un: suddenly he yelled 'House.'

"You've got it Fred?" I said in surprise and delight

"No you dimbo - you have."

I had long ago lost the plot, and had pretty much given up, and looking down at my card with three or four numbers still to rub off, I couldn't believe that Fred had been doing mine as well as his own, and upside down to-boot. He was right of course, and we were presented with the princely sum of £8 for our success. We split the loot and splashed out on a plate of egg and chips. Little was I to know that I was to run into Bingo again many years later on in my life, in the shape of tens of thousands of Bingo cards at Gloucestershire County Cricket Club.

Puerile game? I was grateful then to make a living out of it.

Back at the billet the card school was still in action, but I noticed a stranger in the seat that I usually occupied. He had a pile of loot in front of him, and my four billet mates wore grim losers faces as the cards were dealt.

Soon after I arrived, one of the lads stood up and said, "I'm out," and I asked if I could join in (my 'bank' bolstered by my £4 Housey - Housey success).

To which the stranger said,

"Bugger off, you should have joined in at the start."

"You bugger off Jimmy," said Jock Miller my bedmate, "Sit down Rog."

Matey boy protested, but in vain, and I took my seat.

Fortuitously, I had stood behind 'money- bags' when we got back to the billet, and I had noted how he played, when he held - when he bluffed - how he placed his cards when he had a good hand - and how he bet when his hand was moderate to strong. That, coupled with an amazing run of good cards, I quickly began to reduce matey boys pile to eventually zero.

"That's it then, I'm out" he said at that point, and started to rise, whereupon Jock slammed his hand down heavily on his shoulder and said menacingly,

"What about our money you've got in your breast pocket Jimmy?"

About to argue, matey boy, after staring into Jock's icy blue eyes for a second or two, and no doubt noting the vivid scar, slowly unbuttoned his pocket and produced a fold of £1 and 10/- notes.

"That's better Jimmy. Now let's see if we can get some of our own money back."

It took another hour to clean him out, and although he tried to preserve his 'poke' by not betting, and by stacking early, Jock put the threats on again, particularly when he revealed a small flush that he had stacked early.

"Don't try that again Jimmy. Bet your hand. I'm watching you."

"You can't look at my hand if I stack."

"Who says so – Jimmy?"

"Not according to Hoyle you can't."

"Bugger Hoyle - he was a Yank anyway. We play here according to Jock. Now bet your hand - Jimmy."

The irony of that particular hand was that he would have won the pot if he had played it out.

Finally he was skint, his little wad of notes gone, and Jock allowed him to leave, which he did in some haste, whilst I sat there smiling with a pile of loot spread before me.

I took £5 and the lads split the rest between them. I was the hero of the hour. Hero or not, I could see how the Mafia must operate, and another lesson in life was learned.

Check the house rules first before you play, especially if there is a Glaswegian playing.

One Sunday evening brother Colin, who was home like me for a weekend, and as he was stationed at Yatesbury just a few miles up the road from Compton, was taking me back to camp in his homemade car.

The car was literally homemade. It was a box like structure, but had all the working parts and was of dubious reliability. It did what was asked of it most of the time and was kept in motion by brother's loving attention. However, this Sunday evening the old girl was asked for an exceptional effort when, immediately after driving through a torrential thunderstorm, we rounded a bend in the dark only to be confronted by a lake, and we ploughed straight into it. It was at least two feet deep and the poor old car stopped dead as if running into a brick wall. At the same instant a fountain of water was forced up through the many holes in the floor and thoroughly drenched us both. Fortunately, to the roar of a highly accelerating engine the faithful old machine floated across the lake and found a footing for it's madly revving wheels. Two dripping wet brothers roared with laughter and gratefully drove on.

Brother turned out to be a bit of an inventor, and I often wonder if this old floating 'Tin Lizzie' wasn't the prototype for that thing that appeared in the James Bond movie many years later, that was just as at home in the water as on the road. It was, at any rate, the prototype for another home made car that he built a few years later from a kit that he had bought. It was a red sports car, and he built it in the open air, in the lane in front of our house at Pye Corner.

Another major lesson in life I learned at Compton Bassett, and one that I am ashamed really to recount.

I still can't work out why I did it, but I did.

Most Saturday mornings we were expected to dress up in full uniform including boots, and parade on the camp square. For reasons I cannot recall I decided that I wasn't going to do it. I was determined that I could beat the system and not parade. If I had really engaged my brain I almost surely would have got out of it by pulling the old 'Excused Boots' trick.

But no, I decided that I was going to beat the system.

Pondering a strategy, I used to draw a hoe from the stores and wander about the camp in my denims, so say gardening, before sneaking off early to hitch hike home for a game of football and to see my pretty girlfriend.

One desperately cold Saturday morning I was 'Doing my thing' when I realized that the parade had been cancelled and all the lads were sitting in the nice warm NAAFI drinking tea. They were all looking out of the window and laughing at their dim mate who was frozen to the marrow and clutching his hoe.

I didn't do that again. Which was as well, because soon after, the object of the marching practice became apparent. We were all issued with rifles and were taken down to Calne railway yard in lorries. There we were lined up in readiness to march through the town with our bayonets fixed, before attending a service at the magnificent church.

It was a proud moment for us all, and to think I almost missed it through being such a 'clever dick.'

One little hilarious moment occurred whilst on my skiving Saturday mornings. It started to drizzle with rain and I was wearing my poncho waterproof, when an Officer approached and I threw up a salute only to cover my face with said poncho. What a pratt! Luckily the Officer saw the funny side of it, and I was left to cogitate on my stupidity. That was the second time I had cocked up a salute with an 'Officer on parade.'

One of the lads in my billet was quite an artist and he would decorate our white china mugs for us. Surprisingly, the powers that be turned a blind eye to this provided your mug was pristine clean, and although I shunned a delightful naked lady (which was the most popular by far) I chose to have simply the adage "Roger the Sod from Hambrook" inscribed upon it.

It didn't stop my poor old mug one day feel the wrath of one post bull night inspecting Officer.

"What is that Airman?" said the Officer showing me the inside of my mug that, granted, had the tiniest fleck of tea stain at the bottom.

It was so tiny a blind man would have been glad to see it.

"It's filth Airman that's what it is - filth," and raising his arm above head height, dropped my precious mug, which shattered into a thousand pieces.

"When we have left, sweep that filth up and report to me at lunch time with a new mug."

From memory that little fleck of tea stain cost me 5/- for a replacement from the NAAFI. I do remember that I had no money at that moment and the lads had a whip round and paid for it. My new mug was repainted with my adage and it stayed with me until the day I got home from demob when, as I was unpacking my kit bag, it broke into three. Maybe there was something significant in that. Having carried it halfway around the world, and having it served me well. To end its life in three pieces on the day that I arrived home was perhaps the final severing of the links with service life. But it disappointed me non-the less.

Yet another big, big lesson in life came about at Compton Bassett.

I was placed on Guard Duty (everyone had to do their turn) and I was to Guard the main gates. It was mid winter and bitterly cold and you were more than glad of your greatcoat and woolly gloves I can tell you. There were three of you doing the turn, which was two hours on, four hours off. My stint was 8pm until 10pm and then 2am until 4am.

The first stint was OK as the traffic was busy and I had to check everyone leaving as well as coming in. In fact it was quite fun apart from trying to figure out who was an Officer (you had to salute them) and who was an NCO. But my second stint became a nightmare.

Bitterly cold, deathly quiet, and not a sign of a soul.

An English winter at it's bleakest.

After patrolling up and down for an hour between the gate pillars to try and keep warm, I glanced at my watch to see to my horror that it had stopped at five past two. Hang about, no it hadn't, it WAS five past two. So I patrolled up and down again thinking of home, of my performance as a miserable trainee Wireless Operator, my pretty young girlfriend, in fact a multitude of things, before glancing once more at my watch. Twelve minutes past two. It can't be, there must be something wrong with my watch.

But there wasn't. That's just the way life is sometimes when on guard duty. The middle of the night, in the middle of winter, and there is not another soul in the world alive, and some berk puts you in such a position as this.

I tried everything. I counted the number of bricks in each pillar and (guessing their weight) worked out what each pillar weighed.

My watch said seventeen minutes past two.

I added the weight of the two pillars together and then tried to calculate the amount of cement needed to build them.

I calculated how long it would take one man to build each pillar, firstly on his own and then if he had a mate to mix up the mortar.

My watch said twenty-one minutes past two.

By 3am I was beginning to feel quite strange and becoming confused. Then it dawned on me - I WAS BORED - it was a feeling I had never experienced before, and I can honestly tell you I have never felt since.

I'm glad I did that Guard duty, for without it I would not know just what people mean when they say they are bored - and if they genuinely are - I really feel sorry for them.

Eventually, as I have described, I came to the end of my Wireless Operator's course, and sadly was the only failure in the group. My colleagues, now fully-fledged Wireless Operators were automatically promoted to LAC (Leading Aircraftsmen) and given a £1 a week rise.

I was left dubbed a Telegraphist Assistant (that's a tea boy in civvie language) and still an AC2, and still on 26 bob per week.

We were allowed home for five days leave and were to be informed of our permanent postings on return.

Each day the postings would appear on the Admin. notice board and on day one my pal Fred Nurk drew the short straw - Aden.

We managed to get a swift farewell cuppa in the NAAFI that mid morning before we said goodbye and he was whisked off. I was sorry to say goodbye to Fred. He'd been a really good mate. And we promised to keep in touch.

Others were sent to Christmas Island in the Pacific, which seemed like a Paradise posting at the time. Little did we know that these poor souls were to be part of a nuclear experiment, and to find, as they got older, that they developed Cancer, and few of them made old bones.

A few months of palm trees and hula-hula girls and then…Whoosh!!… 'See you later Alligator.'

"I've got Cyprus" - "I'm off to Singapore." the cries went up creating much excitement.

"You lucky git I've got Norfolk" would be the disappointed wail of one or two.

Germany - Malta - Scotland, the lists appeared but still nothing for AC Plonk Northam - Telegraphist Assistant extraordinaire.

As each lad packed their kit bags and bade their mates goodbye and good luck, the billet swiftly emptied and I, for the first time (and only time in my two years) began to feel a bit lost and lonely. This was a different feeling to when I was left alone when back flighted at Hednesford.

That was punishment of sorts, but this was failure.

Eventually after five days I found myself alone in the billet. Two days passed and on the third, after I had had yet another miserably lonely breakfast, I made my way down to Admin. to see if I had (like dear old Howard at Hednesford) been forgotten.

But no - I hadn't. There on the board, looking alone and unwanted was a solitary card

5019897 AC2 NORTHAM R K
ADEN
REPORT TO POSTINGS ROOM

There I was given details of my posting, fourteen days leave and a rail ticket from Bristol to Gloucester and to report to RAF Innsworth to be issued with tropical kit.

But first they took me to the RAF Hospital at Wroughton where I was given various jabs to combat goodness knows what.

When I told father of my fate, he wasn't too displeased as he had spent a couple of years in Mesopotamia (now Iraq) and thought I might enjoy the desert.

"One thing about it son, the desert will cure you of your Migraines. You will never have another one after being out there. Mespot (as he called it) certainly cured mine. That desert heat thins your blood."

Thankfully he was right. After suffering (sometimes intolerably) terrible Migraines from a baby, which included dreadful nosebleeds and violent nausea and vomiting - headaches that sometimes went on continually for three weeks, and were so bad that I had to be put in a darkened room to at least relieve the discomfort a little - the prospect of 'freedom' from the curse was something I greatly looked forward to. I missed much schooling in my primary days through those headaches, but in those days I suppose they knew little about the causes of the malaise.

So, that posting to Aden - apart from lots of other reasons - has a special spot in my heart.

My family accepted my fate philosophically, but my pretty young Persian Nurse, although she said little was quite unhappy at losing her young man. But she remarked, stoically, 'at least I will be able to study hard and pass my nursing exams.' This she did with distinction, and in fact won all the top awards for her year.

The Silver medal for top nurse - The Matrons prize - and the Hospitals Most Dedicated Nurse award.

I enjoyed my embarkation leave, but it passed all too quickly, and on that last Sunday evening at home, and after kissing mother goodbye, I walked up to the railings on the road with Parvin on my arm to await the bus to Gloucester. Soon after, I heard dad's footsteps coming up the lane and he handed me a fiver saying,

"Don't spend that son until after your next payday - you will probably find that you will need it."

He was more right than he thought, as it was going to be best part of a month before 'The Golden Eagle would shit again.'

FLIGHT TO THE SUN

RAF Innsworth, Gloucester, and with me, a dozen or so Erkies from all over the U.K. - all with their various qualifications from cooks to aircraft fitters - gathered to get kitted out and join the Telegraphist Assistant.

They issued us with tropical gear in the shape of: -

Three khaki short sleeved shirts.

Two pairs of baggy khaki shorts.

Three string vests and three pairs of cotton underpants.

A khaki tie

Three pairs of long woollen knee length socks.

The baggy shorts were very soon tailored to a more acceptable length when we got to Aden. I can't remember who did that work but I think there was a camp tailor (an Arab).

Within days we were up at dawn and bundled into a lorry and taken to the station, to board what must have been the slowest train ever created. We were on that train from 7am until we eventually arrived at Blackbush Airport in Hampshire at 6pm. I could have walked it quicker.

All day with no food or water.

They were building us up for something.

Thankfully, they sat us down in the airport restaurant and gave us the most enormous fry-up on the biggest plate you ever did see. There were thick bacon rashers - kidney - a pork chop - two eggs - fried bread - tomatoes and a generous dollop of baked beans.

Now I hated baked beans. I couldn't stand the smell of them never mind the taste. But I was ravenously hungry and so I decided to close my eyes - hold my nose - and get them down first before I enjoyed the rest of my feast. To my surprise they weren't as unpalatable as I had imagined, although in truth I can't say I enjoyed eating them. Those Blackbush beans, however, largely saved my life, for when I eventually got to Aden the food was almost inedible, and there were times when all I could find to eat was a plate of gooey beans on their (as I called it) Camel-grease fried bread. Funnily enough I actually got to like those Aden beans and even now yearn for that unique taste.

We boarded our plane to the sun, in my case with great

apprehension, as I had never flown before and frankly had no desire to start. It was a four-piston engine Hastings, and to my eyes the puny propellers had little chance of getting its baulk off the ground. My memories of my attempts at aeronautics with Balsa wood and elastic bands as a child, did not fill me with great confidence. But what was it that dad had said,

"You've got to go son - so do your duty with a brave heart."

My 'brave heart' at that moment was in my mouth, but dad wasn't around for me to tell him so.

The (to me) rattletrap of a plane became airborne eventually, and my rigid fear began to disappear as I gazed in wonder at the moonlit clouds below for an hour or so before sleep overcame me.

I was awakened by the rays of the sun streaming through my porthole window, and peering out I could see, through the sparse fluffy white clouds below us, a vast stretch of blue, which turned out to be the Mediterranean.

They hadn't told us - but first stop was to be Malta.

We landed at RAF Luqa and we were whisked off to the mess for another excellent meal. There were about 70 servicemen on the aircraft, made up of an Army Major and about a dozen soldiers, and the rest of us were 'Brylcreem Boys.'

We were told that we would be staying for about 36 hours and we would have to 'doss down' where we could in and around the mess and NAAFI.

The rest of my companions made for the bar, but for me, I wanted to see a bit of Malta if I could, and I strolled out of the gate alone and into the brilliant warm sunshine. Passing a smiling old lady who was surrounded by chickens and a couple of tethered goats, I walked down the hill away from the camp. The air was clean and fresh and I could smell the ocean. I noted that there was a trotting racetrack in the distance at the foot of the hill. There were three or four horses whizzing around the track, pulling their sulkies and drivers and were obviously only practising not racing, as they stopped and started, slowed and then raced away again. Although I wanted to get a closer look, my curiosity in seeing something new for the first time was overridden by my urge to dip my toes in the Mediterranean. I wanted to see the sea and so I turned to my right and made for the smell of ozone.

It was a perfect day, and it was made even more so when I was able to buy two enormous oranges for about 6d the pair from an old Maltese gentleman tugging a hand cart laden to the brim with luscious fruit and vegetables of all kinds. I remember the old man smiled at me and touched my cap badge before pointing to the sky and bowing slightly as he muttered many words that I couldn't fully comprehend other than 'Good - good - thank you - thank you.'

I couldn't help wondering just what he and his family had had to put up with during the war not so many years before.

I sat on a large rock by the cool sea in the warm sun and ate my oranges. They were fresh and sweet and very juicy, and for that couple of hours alone and many miles from all that I loved, I was at peace and I was happy.

The camp cook at Luqa was a Maltese gentleman of extremely jolly nature and gave us (apart from good hearty meals) little tit-bits of food that he had filched from the stores. I particularly remember he was so full of fun and enjoyment of life. He took great delight in showing us how to make a three dimensional four pointed star shape out of moulded bread, and then inviting us to break it by throwing it onto the Terazelled floor. We couldn't manage it as the object instead of splattering into a thousand pieces, simply bounced like a rubber ball.

Another little lesson learned.

Sadly my few hours of Maltese joy were over in a flash and we flew on to Idris in Libya. Here we were off loaded for just two hours or so and given a meal. That meal was pretty basic fare (couscous and stewed lamb) and I remember little of it except thinking, 'if this is what Libyans live on then I'm glad I'm English.'

This 'Cooks tour' to Aden we found out later, was the result of the Suez crisis. At that time the Egyptians would not allow us to over-fly their territories. Personally I was delighted, as it gave me an opportunity to see a bit of the world (albeit briefly) and I was going nowhere was I?

My couple of hours on Libyan soil holds few memories for me other than that where we were looked pretty bleak and was obviously desert, as one might expect being in North Africa, and that it was pleasantly warm.

Our next leg was to be across the mighty Sahara desert to Kano in northern Nigeria, where we were to land in the middle of the night.

As we rattled down the runway on take off, I became alarmed as I noticed that we were long past the airport buildings and that we were still on the deck. I began to have visions of meeting the mountains that I had noticed were situated at the end of the runway, in perhaps a closer manner than I would choose. No one else seemed concerned, but I had made particular note of how long it took to get airborne in our previous two takeoffs and it was much earlier than this.

Eventually we lurched into the sky and with all four engines screaming we cleared the mountains by a good 200ft.

Realising that we must have taken on extra fuel for the long haul south and therefore the old bus must be that much heavier, I breathed a sigh of relief and relaxed as best I could.

As the sun went down, I slept my way across the Sahara.

Kano found me in a completely new world. The soil was rich red in colour, and the tropical gardens of the airport were crammed full of exotic plants and flowers of vibrant reds and yellows. The hot humid air was full of the sounds of insects, and although it was the middle of the night what seemed like highly coloured butterflies (they must have been moths) flitted about in the floodlights. I would guess the temperature was in the 90's, and as the air was still, the sounds and the smells made my head swim. I had just enough time to have a good look around the airport gardens and send mother a postcard before my visit to Nigeria was ended. A pity, for it looked an exciting country.

Two hours later as dawn was breaking, we were airborne again and this time heading East. We flew for some hours over dense tropical forests, the rich canopy only broken occasionally by the odd clearing or small lake or river, before eventually descending and sweeping out over a vast stretch of water, banking hard to our left before gently putting down at Entebbe - Uganda on the edge of Lake Victoria.

We were transferred to two wooden slatted seat RAF buses and driven the forty miles or so through magnificent banana plantations, that sprouted from the rich red soil, to the capital Kampala.

If Malta looked like heaven, to a young village lad, Uganda looked like the Garden of Eden.

On the journey to Kampala we were informed that the soldiers would be taken to an Army barracks and the airmen to an RAF camp on the outskirts of the city. All that is, except me, as I was to accompany the Major to a hotel in the city centre.

The friendly Major and I were given separate rooms on the first floor of this quite luxurious hotel, and I was told to meet him in the bar at 8pm for dinner. The rest of the day was my own.

My room had a separate bedroom with a balcony overlooking a small courtyard which had a large tree growing in the centre of it, and beneath it were half a dozen young African boys having a whale of a time, chattering and laughing, as they threw sticks up into the tree to try and dislodge something or other that I, at that moment, could not discern.

Showered and refreshed I made my way down to the courtyard, to see what the young lads were playing at. Although I couldn't speak their language nor they mine, I quickly learned that they were after the nuts that were ripening on the tree. As I was some sort of expert at removing conkers in their clusters at home, I put my skill to work to the absolute delight of the little boys as shower upon shower of the prized nuts peppered the ground from my well-aimed sticks. I was a hero, and sat in the shade with the boys sharing their bounty. The nuts were delicious and the company delightful.

As I had five or six hours to spare before dinner I wandered down into the town taking in the distinctive African atmosphere. From memory, everyone looked happy (like the children at the nut tree) and prosperous, as well as being distinctly unhurried as they went about their daily lives.

I fell in love with this country immediately.

Little did I know, as I savoured that most delightful moment, that a madman called Idi Amin would ruin this wondrous land in the not too distant future. On reflection, no one could ruin such a place - it was much too beautiful for that.

Feeling rather thirsty, I entered an open fronted bar that had - apart from three noisy Ugandan gentlemen sitting at a table in the corner of the room playing some game that looked like a cross between Ludo and Draughts, but which brought loud roars of laughter at almost every throw of the dice - one solitary smartly dressed Indian gentleman who was sitting on a stool by the bar nursing a large Gin and Tonic.

"Good afternoon" he said in impeccable English, "How very nice to see you."

I was, I must admit, quite taken aback on hearing English spoken for the first time since I had left the Major earlier in the day, and English spoken so beautifully by this rather handsome thirty five year old Indian.

"May I buy you a drink young sir?" he asked politely.

It was at that moment, stupid me, that I realised that I did not have any local currency, whatever it was, just a few English pounds that dad had given me. In fact money, as usual, had not entered my thoughts.

Accepting the man's generosity and then explaining my dilemma he roared with laughter and said,

"Then you drink with me today."

He was most disappointed when I didn't drink alcohol, but was more than happy to order me a very large glass of iced fresh orange juice.

Sadly, I have forgotten his name but he turned out to be the most interesting of characters. He told me that he managed a string of cinemas for his father, and that they were situated all over East Africa. That he owned his own small plane and flew it himself having been taught to fly in the RAF in England just as the war was coming to an end. When I told him I was bound for Aden, he gave me his card and telephone number and absolutely promised to fly to Aden and take me back to Kenya during my leave. He also said that if I liked the life style he would persuade his father to give me a job when my RAF days were over.

Now all of this may have been true, or just 'pie in the sky', but I believed him, particularly when, as he showed me the way back to my hotel, he briefly took me into the foyer of a large cinema where, as we entered, all the staff Kow-towed to him as he showed me around. As I say, I can't remember the gentleman's name, but I do remember the film showing in that luxurious cinema at the time was 'Red River' with John Wayne and the supporting film was a Laurel and Hardy.

Unbelievably, I lost that man's business card, and so a chance meeting in a far off land that might have changed my life for ever, disappeared.

I often wonder if he survived the Amin purge - I really hope so, because if I ever meet him again, I owe him a couple of drinks.

The Major bought me a fruit juice when I met him at the bar at eight o'clock, and we enjoyed a delightful meal together. I ordered a steak and, although it wasn't beef (don't ask me what it was) it was quite delicious. In fact, apart from the wonderful food I have always enjoyed at home, that meal was by far the most memorable that I have ever had.

The Major and I shared sporting stories over our meal, and during our conversation he had noticed that I could not take my eyes off of an enormous reddish brown wicker basket which had a high looped handle, and was piled high with every exotic fruit you could imagine. What particularly caught my eye was a hand of very large (quite twice normal size) red skinned bananas.

"If you would like some fruit then have some" said the Major and asked the waiter to bring the basket. It was so big and heavy it took two to carry it to the table, and when I indicated that I would like one of the red bananas, a plate and sugar and cream were hurriedly provided. The Major chose a very large red apple that would have tempted Snow White. The banana was delicious and tasted somewhat like bakers confectionary custard. I have never seen such a fruit before or since.

Back in the rattletrap, we were now flying over the Ethiopian mountains and from 10000ft (or whatever) it looked a pretty bleak country.

Eventually we were told to 'belt up' as we were about to land in Aden.

I peered out of my porthole and saw below an even bleaker land skirted by the bluest sea in the world. We banked viciously and rounded the 1700ft mountain of Shamsan (Shamsham to us) that stood over the Arab town of Crater City to the south and Steamer Point to the north. Stretching beyond Steamer point was an enormous natural harbour which no doubt was why the British came here in the first place.

It was 11th March 1957.

This was going to be my home for the next fourteen months.

The barren rocks of Aden are without doubt, on first sight, the dreariest most uninspiring vision for the first time visitor, and one could be forgiven initially in wondering what all the fuss was about, and just why an Englishman wanted to be there.

Sixteen thousand troops, a massive airfield, crammed with the latest flying machines. A highly sophisticated tele-communications system et al.

But in the 1950's and 60's this little dot on the map was crucial to the peace and well being of the world, and specifically to the British interests therein. It was situated at the lower end of the red sea and consequently a guardian of the Suez Canal. It was a refuelling and staging post for our (then) considerable navy. And it boasted the most magnificent natural harbour.

It might not have looked much at first sight but it was a very important spot on the map.

In their wisdom the powers that be had sent me there to guard it.

RAF Khormaksar

We landed at Khormaksar airport, and were met by deeply bronzed Airmen, driving their khaki painted RAF buses, and were taken swiftly to camp. The heat was almost unbearable, and the humidity had us all ringing wet with sweat within minutes of disembarking from the plane. And this, they told, us was the Cool season.

The soldiers, poor lads, were sent to live under canvas, whilst we, we were told, could at least look forward to living in purpose built blocks. My first night, however, was spent in a tent in the RAF transit camp, which was situated inside the main gate and to the left but some way from the main buildings.

The latrines at this camp were like something conjured from hell itself.

They consisted of massive 20ft deep pits dug in the sand and the crapper seats were suspended perilously over the stinking fly encrusted morass below. There was over a million flies in that latrine, I know 'cos most of them landed on me whilst I foolishly decided to relieve myself.

Even the Roman Centurions 1500 years before had a better system than this.

Welcome to Aden.

I was told to report the next morning with another lad, to the Signals block, where we stood, white as little lilies, in our spanking new khaki shorts down to just below the knees, and our shining new khaki shirts looking as if they had just been cut from a tent.

With our woollen stockings pulled up to the knee and our berets tucked neatly under our shoulder flap we waited for the gnarled old Warrant Officer to peruse our papers. The pair of us looked for all the world like a couple of refugees from 'It Ain't Half Hot Mum.'

The only thing missing was the pith hat.

After a while he looked up at us and growled,

"Either of you play cricket?"

Now father had told me to never volunteer for anything, but the cricket call had worked at Hednesford, and anyway there was something about this man. I felt instinctively that he was a cricket lover - and he was.

"Yes Sir - I do," I said. Looking at the other lad he ordered,

"Don't unpack your kit son. You're on the plane up country in the morning."

Then looking at me he said,

"What d'you do son, bat or bowl?"

In that instant two young lives were changed forever.

I never saw my colleague again. I found out later that that he was sent to Bahrain Island where they lived in spartan conditions amongst the Arab fishermen, their Dhows, and the local Turtles.

W.O. Stevens became a friend over the next fourteen months. He would, on occasion, engage me in technical cricket talk, and always listened when I passed on some of the wisdoms of the old village cricketers from Hambrook who had taught me so well. He was a cricket 'nut', and in his younger days was a brave man too. He was one of the few Lancaster Bomber rear gunners to survive the war. He occasionally suffered terribly from 'the shakes' which probably accounted for him giving up playing the game that he loved so much: and he took up umpiring. This was a job he did with meticulous perfection. Indeed he insisted at all times that the spirit of the game should be adhered to, and heaven help anyone who did not do so.

I loved the man.

Within a day of being in the burning heat of Aden (and the hot season had not yet begun) I managed to find a bed in Block 5 Bottom West.

There was no one in the billet when I moved in, as the other occupants were all at their duties. The only sign of life was the Arab bearer (servant) who looked after the men and kept their kit and the billet clean. His name was Issam. He said that the bed space was empty and that was good enough for me. Anything to get away from those horrendous latrines.

Just as I was finishing unpacking I was confronted by a giant of a man with blond curls and bronzed muscles bulging out from his scanty shorts and well worn shirt. Handsome bugger he was too.

"You M.T.?" he asked in a strong East Anglian accent. "Because if you're not a driver this is a billet for M.T. boys only" (which turned out to be only 50% true)

"I'm afraid I'm Signals mate. But howdy' do my name is Roger, who are you?"

"Just call me Big Steve - but you can't stay here - so sling your hook."

"Well Big Steve - I'm afraid my hook will not be slung until I find a home, 'cos I'm not going back to those bloody latrines I can tell you."

I smiled at the blonde Goliath, looking him straight in the eye, which I fancy, slightly disturbed him, as he couldn't quite work out if this was a challenge to his authority. Hesitating fractionally he growled,

"Well make sure you do - right."

Big Steve turned out to be a Norfolk farmer's son who (understandably by the size of him) was boss of the billet. When stripped down, his magnificent physique was blemished by a large scar on his left loin where, apparently, he accidentally shot himself as a fourteen year old with a 12 bore shotgun when out rabbiting with his father.

My kit stowed, I went in search of the mess, as I was ravenous. The short walk from the block to the mess taught me a couple of early Aden lessons. I had barely reached the centre of the barren patch between blocks when suddenly, just a couple of yards in front of me, an eerie shape rose from the sand and rushed straight at me bowling me over. It was a mini tornado known as a 'sand devil', and whilst most of them barely reached 6ft tall as they swirled and whirled around before disappearing as quickly as they formed, occasionally they made 10 or 15 feet, and I just happened to catch one of the latter. It didn't hurt me, more shock than anything, but from then on I was much more wary. The other lesson became obvious as I walked on. It was mid-day and there was not a soul in sight. With the sun high overhead, and the temperature soaring to 100f and more, and with the humidity in the order of 100%, by the time I made it to the mess my clothes were ringing wet with sweat, and my appetite diminished. The latter was just as well, for the food was almost inedible.

I remember that meal as though it was yesterday.

Three slices of beef with the edges tinged with green where it had been exposed to the air. A large dollop of 'Pom' (this was dehydrated potato powder) and another dollop of dehydrated mushy peas. A little bit different to that delicious meal I had enjoyed with the Major in Kampala just a couple of days before.

For pudding there was a 4-inch square of what looked like (and tasted like) ships biscuit, swamped with a ladle full of thin yellow tasteless liquid. (I found out later that the liquid was Aden custard).

The sad looking chef - his crumpled hat looking battered and weary - gave me a dull stare.

"Welcome to Aden Moon-man," (all new white arrivals with their pasty white skin were called Moon-men) "Any complaints - tell the Officer."

In fourteen months I only once saw a fresh potato and that was on Christmas Day, and believe it or not we were only then allowed two each.

Eating at Khormaksar became an art form. In the large mess there were half a dozen large fans whirling away from the ceiling, and although they did achieve only a very slight cooling effect, (in truth all they were doing was moving the stifling hot air around from one place to another) should you be lucky enough to sit under one of them, the main benefit was that they kept the myriads of ravenous flies off of your food. This was a benefit of a double kind, for first of all the thought of where those insects had come from (those fly filled latrines were foremost in my mind) and what they might have clinging to their little feet; but perhaps worse than that, they would gobble all your grub down before you got to sit down if you were not alert. Those flies were voracious, you must believe me, and if you were not quick enough getting from the servery to your table they would scoff all of your nosh before you could raise a fork.

Each mealtime the duty Officer would arrive in the mess along with his NCO, but instead of walking around as prescribed, he would take one step inside and shout:

"Any complaints?"

As one, the entire mess would bang their irons on the table and yell back in unison,

"It's shit - shit - it's f......g shit."

To which the Officer would give a curt nod and slight bow and say,

"Carry on Sergeant" and leave.

The first time I heard this I must confess I was shocked and speechless, but realising that it was good for morale, I would on occasion, join in with gusto.

I'm not saying the food was bad - but even the mice in the kitchen brought their own sandwiches.

Our food was bad, but the poor squaddies down the road under canvas had worse. Now and again one would get past the guards and sneak into camp, and when they did we made sure he got some nosh. I remember one emaciated Scot from the Black Watch sitting opposite me, wolfing down his food like a starving man, and eyeing my plate of minced camel (?) 'Pom' and two large leeks, which I had been gazing at in the hope that I could raise the courage to stuff a mouthful down my throat. I was hungry, but not that hungry. I could do no more than push my plate across the table. He gave me a grateful look, said nothing, and within seconds that plate was clean also.

"I owe you pal," he said earnestly.

"No mate, you don't. That's a little thank you for a kindness one of your fellow countrymen showed me once."

He wasn't to know, but the vision of those two little Woodbines lying on my pillow every Wednesday evening, and Jock Miller, was in my mind.

Reporting to the Signals block for duty, I was confronted firstly with my Signals Officer who introduced himself and welcomed me to Aden. He was a pleasant man and who, apart from pay parades, I only ever saw a dozen or so times - he wished me luck and I was then handed over to W.O. Stevens. He quickly explained that the teleprinter section and telephone exchange were grossly understaffed and that he wanted me to 'fill the gaps' until fresh faces were sent out from the U.K.

Even though I had no choice in the matter, I was more than happy to help out, particularly as the Signals block was one of the few places on the camp that had air conditioning.

Air-conditioned and bomb proof.

The small operational block was surrounded by granite walls that sloped inward on the outside and outward on the inner. All designed to deflect blast. The top of that wall was flat and about four feet wide and some feet above the operational block roof, and sitting on top of it one had a fabulous view of the airfield. I spent many happy hours up there during my breaks watching our brave young pilots going about their duties. The airstrip was used for civilian traffic too, but that was sparse and it was mainly the RAF lads zipping in and out. And a very busy airstrip it was too. It was here that I witnessed one day, a most remarkable feat of flying by one of our lads.

The entire Ethiopian Air Force had come over on a 'Show the Flag' occasion and our boys put on an Air Show for them.

The Ethiopian's, poor souls, flew about a dozen or so Tiger Moths and must have been most impressed with our state of the art force, which included, Venom fighters, Valiant bombers, Valetta's, plus the impressive Beverley transporter.

After the compulsory fly past, it was left to our 'flying ace' to show what he could do. He flew his Venom high up into the clear blue Yemen skies, spinning and looping and making the little fighter almost talk. Finally he came screaming down in an almost vertical dive, before, at the runways end, flipping the aircraft onto its back, and flying the entire length of the strip upside down barely twenty feet off the deck.

The man must have been mad. But one thing is for sure it made thrilling watching, and I thought at the time, I bet the Ethiopian's will think twice before invading us!

My first few days in the Protectorate were hectic as you can imagine, but in between sorting myself out and finding out where everything was, I set about in earnest trying to locate my old mate Fred Nurk.

After getting nowhere with my initial enquiries, I decided that as this place was a great deal bigger than I had imagined, what with all the stations up-country and all, I would give it one last go at finding him by searching billet by billet. Few people worked after mid-day as it was so hot, and they usually spent the afternoon lying on their 'pit' resting. So I set out in my quest. Fortuitously I chose the correct block to start. As I entered the billet on the middle floor of the block next to mine, I was overjoyed to see, down at the far end and sitting on his bed with his back to me - my man.

He didn't see me coming and only looked up as I stood at the bottom of his bed. When he saw me, his face was a picture. For a moment he really was in a bit of a pleasant shock, and we both stood there smiling at each other before he stood and embraced me. Of course he had no idea that I too would be sent to Aden, and he must have wondered if we would ever meet again.

It was good to see the old boy once more.
Within a week or so, a bed became vacant in my billet, and Fred moved in to Block 5 Bottom West. He told me afterwards that his couple of weeks prior to seeing me had been a bit lonely and that he was missing his Compton Bassett days.

He was working out of the control tower on the airfield and not enjoying it overly, although they were very busy. It was a job, however, that he only did for a short while before being moved down to the Maala Straight, where he became one of the privileged Wireless Operators that worked on the Motor Torpedo Boat that the Air Sea Rescue used.

ON GUARD

W.O. Stevens told me that he was putting me into the Teleprinter Room, and that I was to be under Corporal Butterworth, who would tell me what was what.

"Well that's got that out of the way lad. Now lets get down to the real business in hand," he said smiling broadly.

He quizzed me closely on my cricketing experience, and said that he was hopeful that we (Signals) might put up a good show in the coming season that was just about to start. We have a captain he explained, but he believed his team should be captained by consensus, and that any input I could offer would be welcome. This idea, incidentally, I did not agree with, but agree or not, I wasn't about to queer my pitch with the 'WO - man' until I saw how the land lay. And anyway, his idea might work.

In the event his 'democratic captaincy' idea worked quite well, and we had a very successful season.

Corporal Butterworth was a slightly built man and perhaps a little insignificant physically, but his strong character, and honest manner more than compensated for his lack of size. He was a good 'boss' and ran his Signals office immaculately and efficiently. He welcomed me to 'hell' (as he put it) and introduced me to my workmates. Two of them were Welshmen, and both fine lads. Rod Hamill was from Llanelli and a most handsome man. Talented on the teleprinter was Rod but also an extremely talented actor and particularly as a man of humour. We were soon to team up as a double act and wow the troops. Bruce 'Taffy' Nash came from Barry and enjoyed being on the stage, and as it so happened, he was at that very time in the process of producing a Variety show that was to be staged in the camp open air cinema (The Astra) over two nights, just two weeks away. The third member of the team was a lad who I believe came from Birmingham, but he was soon to depart for England having finished his tour.

Corp. B. pulled me to one side and explained that Signals had been assigned some guard duties. Guard duty was not normally given to anyone who worked night shifts (which we did in Signals) as we had to man our positions 24 hours per day, seven days a week; but for some reason the camp needed extra guards and we all had to weigh in.

As we were desperately short of trained men, and as I was an untrained, failed Wireless Operator, he asked if I would mind doing all of the guard duties allocated to us until reinforcements came from the U.K.

Although having only been in Aden a couple of days I had already learned that guard duty in this part of the world was not only dreadfully uncomfortable because of the heat and humidity, but could be downright dangerous, as the rebel tribesmen of the Yemen were apt to make the odd sortie looking for ammo and explosives.

My new mates eyes told all as I said,

"No problem Corp. - you can count on me."

"Great" said the relieved NCO; "I shall more than make it up to you I promise."

So it was that I, moon-man as I was, found myself doing two or three guard duties every week for the next six weeks.

Fortunately for me, we were soon to have extra help arrive from the U.K., and Corporal B. was true to his word when it did arrive. It was about this time also that Signals were relieved of their Guard duties anyway, and so the pressure was really off.

"Right Rog." he said at that happy time, "Unless there is illness or an emergency, you can come in when you want. In fact you needn't come in at all if you don't feel like it."

From then on I was pretty much my own man regarding work, and although I did help the lads out with night shifts etc., and helped relieve the pressure in the telephone exchange, it meant that I had lots of free time for my sport and for my script writing. All those guard duties certainly paid off.

Even then, most of those were not so bad. Obviously the duty Officers and the military police (Snowdrops) soon got to know me, and were generally most sympathetic when allocating duties. I almost always got the 'soft ones.'

Not so my first night on guard.

The very next day I was to report to the Guardroom at 6pm suitably dressed, as I was to be on Bomb Dump duty that night. When I told my new colleagues back at the billet what duty I had been assigned to, a sudden deathly hush fell over them. One by one they shook their heads and with looks of sympathy rolled over on their 'pits.'

Remember, none of these fellows knew anything about me as I had only just arrived, so I thought perhaps they were all being just a touch unfriendly.

"What's up?" I asked, not without a little alarm, for I must admit I had thought that 'Bomb Dump' had sounded a bit intimidating.

"Nothing" said a gnarled old lorry driver with skin the colour of walnut.

"I've been out here eighteen months and we've lost nine men so far on Bomb Dump guard. You'd better keep your eyes peeled or that bed will be vacant again."

Not one prone to fear under normal circumstances, this time I couldn't help wanting detail.

"What d'you mean 'lost'?" I enquired.

"You know - lost" he replied running his fingers across his throat.

"Good luck Moon-man."

We were loaded into the back of a lorry having been issued with a rifle and a clip of five rounds of live ammunition, a whistle, and a large bottle of water.

We were told that under no circumstances were we to load our rifles unless specifically ordered to do so.

Then we drove off into the darkness.

There was no moon, just a myriad of twinkling stars - and we drove through the pitch darkness for miles.

What I did not know was that this was an elaborate hoax set up just for me.

The Duty Corporal and the other two lads were in on the 'joke' and the M.T lorry driver had deliberately gone around and around in wide circles in the darkness of the night to give the impression that the Bomb Dump was way out in the desert, 'for safety sake' as the Corporal put it. To someone just two days into desert duty it all seemed plausible enough.

Off-loading alongside a quite forbidding mountain of bombs that was surrounded by a ten-foot high wall of sandbags, the NCO allocated our two-hour watches. Mine was to be 10pm until midnight and 4am until 6am.

We had for shelter a small permanently erected tent containing two beds. Neither bed had a mattress, just springs, but, as the Corporal pointed out,

'At least it will keep the scorpions off of you.'

I didn't envisage getting too much sleep keeping watch for scorpions.

We had a game of cards and made a brew on a little primus stove and introduced ourselves. The other lads were 'old sweats' and had been in Aden for a year or more, and they tried to reassure me that as long as I kept my eyes peeled and ears open during my shift, things should be all right.

I said little, but wondered just how we were going to keep our eyes peeled in the absolute pitch darkness.

When my turn came around, I did my statutory one circuit of the giant pile of bombs, rifle over my shoulder, before I caved in to my anxiety and loaded my, now miserably inadequate looking, clip of five bullets into my comforting weapon. For extra safety sake I slipped one up the breach.

I knew I was breaking serious orders, but bugger it man, I was a little bit scared.

Those of you who have done such guard duties will know that time really does stand still on such occasions, and as I made my slow third circuit around those lethal bombs (enough to blow the whole of Saudi Arabia to kingdom come I reckoned), with my eyes popping out of my head as I strained to 'keep them peeled' I suddenly froze in fear.

I could hear voices - in the distance admittedly - but yes, there was an occasional muffled voice and with it a faint creaking of what sounded like a wooden cart.

I stood motionless - ears straining.

What to do? Do I call the Corporal?

Yes that's it - I need help.

At that precise moment I came close to dirtying my underwear as I heard the sound of a bolt action of a rifle in very close proximity.

Terrified (and I mean terrified) but now icy cool, I readied my weapon. As I aimed carefully at the moving shadow not 30ft away from me and began to (as taught) gently squeeze the trigger, a lighter flashed into life revealing a grinning (and almost dead) Corporal.

"Want a fag Rog" he chuckled, and strolled across the gap in the sand bags to let me in on the jape.

In truth I was too scared to tell him that I was holding a loaded rifle and that I had come within an ace of shooting him.

He explained all.

The voices and cart sounds were real enough, they came from a camel train that came down from Sheik Othman - up country - and were on a road some two or three miles away, but as the desert was flat and featureless the sounds they made carried on the still night air, making them appear to be much closer at hand.

He told me also of the 'long drive' in the lorry, and that we were but at the edge of the Khormaksar runway not half a mile from the camp. We could see no lights as a high sand bank had been built between the camp and the bombs for safety reasons.

It was all a big jape, and half the camp were waiting to hear how it all panned out. Thankfully it all ended well and not in the disastrous manner my disobeying of strict orders might have made it, with me having killed an innocent man through my cowardice, and he dead simply for playing an elaborate practical joke.

In a way I am glad that the lads played their little trick on me, for it was the first time in my life that I had ever experienced real fear, and indeed I have only ever experienced fear once since that night in the desert, and that was whilst playing cricket - but that's another story.

SIGNALS BLOCK

My job at the Signals block initially, was sorting out the busy incoming traffic to its rightful pigeonhole before it was passed on to its appropriate home. More importantly, my main job was to make the tea (chai).

The daytime shifts were hectic as we were taking traffic from the whole of the Saudi Arabian area which consisted of half a dozen or so units based right around the coast, including Bahrain Island, Sharjah, Masira Island, Salala and Dhala, besides some from Habbaniya-Iraq, and East Africa.

All U.K. traffic came to us first before we distributed it to its correct destination. Quite a lot of the traffic was of the 'Top-secret' variety as there was a war going on quietly, and men were regularly losing their lives in this desolate place. Few in the U.K. were aware of it, and few cared.

The night shift, however, was very quiet, and it gave me an opportunity to learn to type on the teleprinter. Very quickly I became quite proficient, albeit only using two fingers and a thumb on each hand. Typical me, self taught at everything, and so not able to reach the dizzy heights of excellence at anything, as I never learned to do a thing entirely correctly. You should see my swimming strokes, or better still my golf swing to see what I mean. Unique or what?

However, I could soon type pretty fast and accurately, and right at this moment as I type this now, I can thank my quiet Aden nights for it.

The lads were grateful that I was about, and Corp. B, as I have said, especially so.

"I will make it up to you Rog. I promise - you wait and see." he kept saying.

I didn't mind - I was going nowhere was I?

The days were flashing by and that air conditioning was doing my prickly heat the world of good. It didn't stop me losing weight though. Lean as I was when I arrived in Aden, within six weeks I had lost almost a stone and would barely have made a middleweight in the fight game.

One of the replacements was a well built, though slightly tubby, freckled faced, fair-haired lad who came from South Shields. Although he was forewarned about the heat, he chose to ignore the advice and on his first day off decided to go for a walk around the camp without his shirt. He was gone for barely an hour and turned up at the signals office looking decidedly unwell. He had gone a terrible raw red colour, and as the afternoon progressed large (very large) yellow blisters began to appear all over his podgy torso. His face also was swelling up, and we had to call an ambulance and get him rushed to hospital. There he was kept in for two or three weeks with third degree burns. He recovered eventually, but then found himself on a 'Fizzer' for self-inflicted injury.

He was a very good footballer, as it happened, and had played centre half for South Shields Boys during 1953, the same year as I was playing centre half for Bristol Boys. He took over the defending spot from me in the Signals team, and I then played inside forward. It helped a bit, but our team was pretty ordinary and we didn't win many games.

Very soon I was taken into the telephone exchange in the room next door and shown how to work that. During the busy morning shift it took two operators to handle the madly flashing monster.

It was one of those old fashioned jobs that you see in the old time movies where you had to wear earphones and carry a speaker tube on your chest. The switchboard consisted of eighty numbered holes (the camp extensions) into which you plugged a wire to connect one extension to the other. Each hole had a light above it, which lit when the handset in that particular office was lifted. Obviously it went out when the call was over and the handset returned to its holder.

I can tell you, when it was busy, that little room was lit up like Blackpool illuminations, and to work it with efficiency and at speed was quite mentally exhausting. I must have said the words 'Number please – Hold the line – Trying to connect you' a million times and more, and all said (hopefully) without a trace of boredom and in a pleasant manner. This experience stood me in good stead when years later I had to teach my girls at Gloucestershire County Cricket Club how to answer the phone and encourage business.

Nothing would irritate you more than some ignoramus flicking his handset bar up and down in impatience if you kept them waiting. If you weren't careful that rattling handset bar would burst your eardrum. One could retaliate by holding the 'bell key' on alert when the 'rattler' was talking, sending a piercing buzz back to rattle his eardrums Some of them never seemed to learn however, so the 'war' went on.

Once I gave the perpetrator a right bollocking for flashing his handset, only to find it was the Group Captain Commanding Officer.

How was I to know he had visited the M.T. maintenance hangar that day and needed to make an urgent call?

To be fair he apologised, and what's more, within a few days paid us an unscheduled visit and apologised to my face. He was surprisingly interested in the exchange and just how busy it was.

I became quite proficient at it (it wasn't difficult you could train a Chimpanzee in a couple of days) but I must say I was more than glad to slip back into the teleprinter room and the relative peace. Often though, I would take my mug of chai into the telephone exchange and give my mates a ten-minute break on a busy morning. These lads really did appreciate what I did, and Corporal B. took my advice when I suggested that short bouts of relief produced a smoother and better switchboard during 'rush hours', and he tried to rearrange the shift pattern wherever he could.

When I was on permanent telephone duty there were a couple of times where I had to down tools and climb up onto the wall for ten minutes and watch the planes fly in and out, or I would have gone crackers.

It's a wonder to me that more switchboard bods haven't lost it in the past.

There were three or four outside lines on the board that were used for overseas calls, plus an emergency telephone box close to the married families blocks. Now this emergency phone simply stood on its own, looking not unlike the telephones you see at the side of Motorways. No phone box - just a lonely pole with its handset perched on the top.

The night shifts brought extra fun from both those outside lines and that lonely emergency phone.

The married families line was often visited on an evening time, by a young officers daughter who was having an illicit liaison with an Indian gentleman at Steamer Point. I admit to my shame now, that we used to listen in to their, often lurid, conversations. The young lady was always most punctual with her calls and would lift the receiver and politely request her lovers number. Unbeknown to her we would set up half a dozen phones in the block and the

'Snowdrops' would come around for a chai and a listen in. It was all good harmless fun, but not really a fair way of using the exchange.

If the poor girl had known that there was a dozen or so lecherous young airmen sharing her secrets she would have been mortified.

The Hospital switchboard at Steamer Point was manned by WAAF'S, and from time to time we used to ring them up in the middle of the night for a chat. Although they were all dating Officers and so right out of our reach, they were good fun, and kept us boys entertained during the long nights. Chatting to young ladies on the telephone can play havoc with your imagination, and when I was hospitalised with dysentery some time into my stay in Aden, it was an amazing (though very pleasing) sight to see my favourite 'telephone WAAF' walk into the ward with a get well card from the girls, and she being all of fourteen stone and not unlike Hattie Jacques to look at. In my imagination, as we used to chat during those night shifts, she was quite a petite little thing. But fourteen stone or not, it really was a thoughtful thing to have done to visit a miserable sick airman miles from home and his mum.

There were only a couple of dozen single females in Aden, and about sixteen thousand troops, if you counted the army, and so you can see I was both lucky and privileged to come into contact with the opposite sex through my show biz work and the telephone exchange.

It doesn't take a lot of imagination to see how important the cinema was to the troops. To most of them it was the nearest they ever got to the fairer sex.

I particularly remember one day when I saw my same Florence Nightingale lass, all fourteen stone of her, sitting on the sands in her swimsuit at Elephant Bay, surrounded by twenty or so love lorn lads all gazing at her as though she was Marilyn Monroe.

THE BIG SHOW

Taffy Nash, as I have said, was in the throes of producing a Variety Show to be performed in the open air cinema on camp just a couple of weeks after my arrival. On hearing this, I asked if he had a comedian, and when he said that he did not have a stand-up as such, and that the humour was to be provided by a series of sketches, I volunteered my services. Initially my offer was greeted with great caution. I could understand his reluctance to a degree. The show was due on in less than two weeks and they had been rehearsing for ages. He was happy with it so why change it. But I pressed him hard, telling him that my spot would not interfere with any of his rehearsed work. Eventually, and reluctantly, he gave in and said,

"Come along to rehearsals tomorrow evening, and we will listen to your act."

"I'm afraid not old chap - my gags will be all over Aden by the time I go on - and I will die the death."

Taff could not see this, but then perhaps he wasn't as experienced as he professed. This was proved when he eventually said,

"Alright then, I will give you a six minute spot to open the show. Bring me in your act for me to read."

I wrote out my act, which took him just six minutes to read, and after timing it carefully, he gave me the nod.

I opened the show all right, but of course Taff's inexperience showed when my six minutes became twenty minutes. When you added in the laughter (thankfully) and repartee with the audience your act can last forever.

I came off the stage that first night soaking wet with sweat, and exhausted with elation and burned out adrenalin.

The second night I was 'Top of the Bill.'

Less than three weeks into my Aden tour and it seemed everybody knew me.

There was one lovely little occurrence to boost my ego. After the second night, as the show ended, a lady was waiting outside the stage door and said to me,

"I saw you in a show at Blackpool last summer didn't I? But I can't remember your name."

Flattered as I was I couldn't let the deception continue, and I explained to her that it wasn't me that she had seen. She walked away unconvinced, but it left me feeling quite pleased with myself.

The show itself was excellent and as good as some of the ENSA groups that came out later.

Taff Nash enjoyed entertaining, as did my other fellow signaller Rod Hamill, and we decided to form a cabaret group to entertain the troops and their families. Taff persuaded the talented Margaret Sowerby to join us, and we made our debut at the Families Club that was situated on camp.

Sadly, soon after our first performance Taff was hurriedly called home, and given a compassionate discharge. There had been a death in the family, and he was needed to run the family business.

It was then that The Pentagons were born.

THE PENTAGONS

With Bruce Nash now gone home and Rod and Margaret keen to do more entertaining, we decided to persuade Bobbie Campbell and Fred Nurk to join us.

There were now five of us, and so, perhaps not too originally, we decided to call ourselves The Pentagons.

The Five of us we were made up of Rod and myself, Bobbie (jock) Campbell who was an M.T. driver and a pal of Rod's, and my old mate Fred Nurk (Bernard O'Donaghue). The fifth member of the group was the very pretty Margaret Sowerby. I can tell you, when the five of us were gathered together at rehearsals, there was a real mix of accents.

There was Roderick with his lilting Llanelli Welsh, Fred with his Cockney patter, me with my West Country burr, Margaret with her beautifully modulated English, and Bobbie with his strong Glaswegian drawl. At times there was a genuine call for an interpreter. But it all added to the fun of being together. Sometimes Bobbie would come out with an expression that left us baffled, and I well remember one day when he used the term 'Burrell.' When I asked him to translate he replied. "You no ken what a burrell is? A burrell is a terrrum for a turrrn."

Rod and I found that we worked well together as a double act. People loved us, which wasn't surprising as Rod was one of the funniest men that I ever met. His timing was impeccable and his 'feel' for an audience quite extraordinary. I used to write the scripts, but once Rod had the bare bones of my efforts, he could add a word here, or a raised eyebrow there, and turn quite ordinary stuff from my pen into magic humour. There were times when I was so convulsed whilst on the stage with him that I struggled to keep up with the plot. It didn't matter, we seemed to know exactly what each other was going to say or do. Having said that we did rehearse quite a lot.

We were very lucky when the very pretty Margaret Sowerby asked to join our little group. Margaret played the guitar and sang very well as did her older sister Maureen. In that earlier Variety Show in The Astra, the two girls performed as a double act and really wowed the lads. Having the pretty, sweet smelling Margaret with us, as one fifth of The Pentagons, made us the envy of the whole camp.

Margaret was a perfect young lady, full of fun and exuberance and behaved impeccably. She was a credit to herself and her parents.
Sadly she was to leave us at the end of 1957 to return to England with her father. But not before she had worked as a stewardess on the leave flights to Mombasa. Margaret was a very pretty and talented young lady and, if she so wished could have made her name in show business.

Both Rod and I had our beautiful young ladies at home, but it was still a wonderful pleasure to have Margaret around us.

One evening her mum and dad (Squadron Leader Sowerby) invited us four lads to a party at their house, (I think it must have been one of the girls birthday) which was situated right at the end of the Khormaksar runway. There was just the five of us Pentagons plus Margaret's sister Maureen.

Mrs Sowerby supplied some sumptuous food and the Squadron Leader copious amounts of ice-cold beer and coke. The parents left us alone to enjoy one another's company. Perhaps surprisingly, as the price of alcohol was so low in the NAAFI, none of us lads were drinkers. Although an occasional beer would be taken: we were 'coke' drinkers by and large.

The girls wanted us to hear the latest 'pop' music that was fresh out of the U.K., which had been brought out by one of their dad's colleagues. I seem to remember their particular excitement with the latest acquisition, an L.P. of 'West Side Story.' (Or was it 'My Fair Lady?').

That evening Rod and I managed to frighten them both to death with personal tales of our experiences with ghosts. Some of the stories had a grain of truth in them but most were figments of our fertile imaginations. Goodness knows how this subject got brought up, but do I remember they were both so scared.

I bet they didn't sleep that night.

The Pentagons had much fun entertaining anyone who would listen. Our set, apart from Margaret of course, was almost exclusively humorous. I would compere the show and also do a solo comedic spot. Rod and I would perform our double act, and Margaret sang beautifully to her own guitar accompaniment. She could sing any kind of song but preferred skiffle or country and western. We would mime to a number of Stan Freeburg records, and this meant that Bobbie and Fred were able to perform without showing their nerves too much. Bobbie in particular began to enjoy his new found fame, and we had many hilarious rehearsals. Fred's solo spot was miming to Stanley Holloway's famous 'Albert and the Lion.' He eventually got so confident that he would, on occasion, do it 'live'.

For an encore he would slip in 'Sam, Sam Pick Up Thee Musket.'

As a group our speciality (this was Rod's brilliant idea) was 'dancing' to some of the hits of the day, to Rod's brilliant choreography. A big favourite with the desert audiences was our rendition of that real old favourite 'The Old Bazaar in Cairo.'

I must say when we donned our Fez's dear old Fred looked made for the part.

The star spot of the show was Rod's Boris.

We had created a couple of wonderful characters that gave Rod free reign for his talents. There was Pricilla; a shy virginal young lady that was a particular favourite of the lads, especially when she lifted her pretty skirt to reveal Roderick's hairy legs. But popular as she was, everyone's favourite, and star of every show, was Boris - a simpleton who was forever in trouble.

Boris was a cross between Jerry Lewis and Walter Mitty and would spend his time on stage annoying me as I went about my business of introducing the next item or attempting a 'serious' rendition of 'say' 'The Charge Of The Light Brigade'

Rod's Boris was a very funny character that would bring the house down, anywhere, even to this day.

We would be delighted when we were rewarded with handfuls of East African money (the currency in Aden) for our efforts. But we enjoyed it so much we would probably have performed for nothing.

Later on, when we were both demobbed, Rod and I had auditions for the BBC and also for the local commercial TV station TWW.

The BBC audition took place in the old Bristol Empire theatre (now demolished) and Rod and I were in awe of the fact that we were using the same dressing rooms and treading the same boards as all of those fantastic stars of yesteryear. Laurel and Hardy being almost certainly the most famous of all the acts that performed there, and Rod and I felt privileged to be, probably, the last 'Double Act' to follow in their illustrious footsteps. Wonderful performers graced that stage, from Max Miller to Rob Wilton. My mother used to fill my head full of the tales of the stars that she saw there including her particular favourites Marie Lloyd and Randolph Sutton. Indeed, I was taken there to see pantomimes and the odd variety show as a very young child, and I loved it.

Full houses for those stars in those days, but for our performance there was just an audience of five.

As we intended to do a little song and dance in our twelve-minute spot we had asked Rose Lloyd (now Ewens) to come down and play for us. She was as thrilled as us to have walked out onto that famous old stage.

Finishing our twelve minutes (which was more than most of the other acts managed before they got the dreaded 'Thank you - we'll let you know') we were asked for a little more, to our delight. After we had completed a little extra we were called down into the auditorium to speak to the adjudicator.

"Boys" he said, "You have much talent, but you are as raw as one can be. If you have a season at Butlins, (and I can give you the phone number of a man to ring to arrange it) and then come and see me in the autumn, I will guarantee you work."

Then turning to Rod he said with an impish grin,

"You are a naturally a very funny man - have you ever considered getting a new partner?"

Noting my crestfallen look he patted me on the arm,

"I was only joking son. The pair of you work together brilliantly."

We never did join Butlins. Rod went back to marry his Sybil in Llanelli, and to continue his work as an electrician, and I went back to my Parvin and started to search for my destiny.

As the years have passed and I have watched double acts come and go, I absolutely know that Rod and I could have made it to the top if we had stuck at it. I have no regrets however, as I have had a wonderful life and enjoyed quite a bit of success on the stage as a part time professional comedian when I was younger.

GOODBYE HEADACHES

Six weeks into my Aden tour and I had lost best part of a stone in weight, and suddenly I realised that my headaches were gone. So perhaps dad was right after all. Thankfully it turned out that he was, and to this day I have never had another Migraine attack.

My time in Aden was crammed full of interest. I played football for the Signals team and although we were not very strong and struggled a bit to even win a match, I enjoyed it despite the heat. Football was played in the 'Cool Season' when the temperatures were around 80f to 90f, and was played on hard rolled out sand. It was more like shale really, and you didn't want to go down on it if you could help it. The Signals cricket team was much stronger, and we did very well, winning all (or most) of our matches. Cricket was played in the 'Hot Season' with temperatures reaching 120f, and was played on the football pitch. Obviously the goalposts were removed, and a coconut matting wicket laid in the centre. The matting wicket played remarkably well and encouraged stroke play. With a boundary line of a good eighty to ninety yards the fielding side were helped in their efforts to keep the boundaries down. The matting wicket played very well and suited my batting to a tee.

My cricket produced a number of extraordinary matches and these I have written down in my book "66n.o. – Tales of a Village Cricketer."

We swam a bit, mainly in the sea at Elephant Bay which was situated the other side of Steamer Point and which boasted a shark net. The sea was warm and clear blue, and full of multicoloured fish. There were groups of coral to wonder at, and without doubt it was one of the big bonuses of being in Saudi Arabia.

Alongside the Astra was the camp open-air swimming pool, which I hardly ever used. Within the first couple of weeks of arriving on the camp, a dozen or so of us made our way to the pool, one evening in the pitch darkness, for a swim. It was forbidden to use the pool after dark, and as it turned out we were to soon find out why. The lad in front of us ran on ahead whooping. He ran along the springboard and dived in only to find that someone had emptied the pool.

He was pretty badly hurt with a broken wrist and arm and a seriously smashed head. I never liked that pool after that, although, like the sea at Khormaksar beach, on certain nights of the month, when you dived in a bright flash of phosphorescence lit the water. It was quite a spectacular sight and worth risking a few days' jankers for if caught.

I preferred to travel down to Steamer Point and Elephant Bay for a swim. It was, relatively, a long way to go, but at least there was a nice beach and the sea was full of colourful fish and exotic coral. There was also a man made open-air swimming pool at Elephant Bay and the Command swimming Gala was held there. I attended one Gala and can remember vividly a Johnny Weissmuller (Tarzan) look-alike sweeping the board in all the races. I have forgotten his name but I understand that he had represented Great Britain in the freestyle at the Commonwealth Games or some such tournament. I do recall him powering up and down that pool creating a bow wave and leaving everyone else in his wake.

The weather itself was pretty boring, in as much as, every day without fail the sun poured down out of a clear blue sky scorching the sand and anyone foolish enough to stand out in it. We were warned that it was our responsibility to not get sunburn, or worse, sunstroke, and that it was a chargeable offence to do so. Twice a year the sun passed overhead as it made its way first to the Tropic of Cancer, and then back on its way to the equator and the Tropic of Capricorn. The proximity of the Indian Ocean created almost 100% humidity, which persisted day and night. The mere act of breathing made you sweat, and it was essential you kept taking the salt tablets that were liberally supplied. I couldn't get on with them. They made me nauseous, and so I made sure I put a little extra salt on my food. A habit I still have to this day, and the cause of my high blood pressure they say.

Very occasionally a small fluffy white cloud could be spied floating up from the south. As if by magic it would hone in on Shamsan's peak, and on arriving, simply sit there for a while before dissipating, seemingly, in moments.

I only saw it rain twice in fourteen months. Once it lasted for 8 or 10 minutes and didn't even wet the sand. The other time, however, it was quite different. It rained for an hour or more - and did it rain. It came down in torrents, and dead straight, like curtain rods. In no time at all everywhere was flooded to the depth of several inches, and one could see how those dried up Wadis came about. They were the result of such torrential rain and flash floods that gouged conduits out of the sand. The whole of the camp became a lake, and we enjoyed standing out in the rain taking an unexpected but enjoyable fresh water shower. I remember how surprised I was that the rain was actually warm. Within a couple of hours the lake had disappeared and the merciless sun was back to dry out the sodden Yemeni sand.

I swore that I would never again complain about rain when I got home, and, apart from cricket days, I never have.

Moonlit nights were a sight to behold as the Yemeni moon seemed twice the size of ours back home, and the light from it matched some of the midday November light in England.

The moon's features were so clearly defined as the enormous orb floated almost within touching distance.

What with the magnificent stars on moonless nights being such a crystal clear marvel, with every single star seemingly almost within arms length, and that enormous glowing moon, I could see how and why our ancestors of long ago could be so overawed.

On a new moon night the seas around Aden produced another natural display to wonder at. The entire ocean glowed with phosphorescence. It was quite spectacular. I am sure it must occur in other parts of the world, but I felt privileged to have witnessed it. We used to wander down to Khormaksar beach on such nights and just stand quietly and enjoy the wonder.

Khormaksar beach must be one of the largest in the world. It was a couple of hundred yards wide and about 500 miles or more, long, as it stretched northward to the Muscat of Oman. For some reason (a reason that I couldn't fathom) there appeared to be little or no tide. Often we would go down to this magnificent beach to play football. We never swam or even paddled in the water, as the sea was quite shallow and one would need to wade out a long way to find sufficient depth to swim, and anyway the sea was infested with sharks and poisonous jellyfish. Tale had it that the previous (to my tour) C.O.'s wife whilst wading out in the sea, lost part of her leg to a shark, and was only saved by her Arab bearer who was able to scare off the predator before dragging her to safety.

As I have explained earlier, we did swim in the sea, but this was at Elephant Bay - Steamer Point, where there was a shark net in place. On one such trip whilst diving down to get closer to the coral and the fishes, Rod obtained a small scratch on his calf which within days turned poisonous, and hospitalised the old boy for a week or so. I bet he still retains that vicious scar that that little nick left behind.

It was on Khormaksar beach that I had two searing memories for life. The first will seem insignificant in the telling, but it was an excruciating experience for me, and something I would not wish upon anyone.

I was playing barefoot football with the lads when I was overtaken with severe stomach pains. I needed to get back to the billet quickly, and so I set off, half running, to cover the mile or so. It was a route that took me through the area where the married families lived, and then across the open sports ground.

Block 5 - my home - was the block farthest away but one, and although it was in sight, it seemed a hundred miles away to me at that moment. I quickly realised that I had Aden tummy and a nasty accident was on the cards if I didn't hurry. The problem was that I couldn't. As I hurried along, the control of my bowels became extremely difficult, and every twenty yards or so I had to stop to contain myself. I suspected that I might have dysentery, which is contagious, and so I certainly didn't want to use anyone else's loo and perhaps give it to them.

No - I just had to make it back home

That journey took forever.

How I didn't soil myself I know not, but, thank God, I eventually made it. The final 200 yards were made in 2 to 3 yard bursts. I wouldn't wish that experience on a dog. It turned out to be dysentery, and I was hospitalised for 10 days at the Military Hospital at Steamer Point.

The other Khormaksar beach experience was completely different, and in it's way even more unforgettable.

We were playing football once again, when one of the lads yelled out,

"Look out lads - duck." and pointed northward up the beach.

Now Khormaksar beach, as I have described before, was wide and flat and long, and stretched into the distance for 500 miles or more toward Oman and the Persian Gulf.

There in the distance was a Valiant bomber hurtling towards us at what, at that moment, appeared to be an altitude of zero feet. At first glance it appeared to be crashing or at the very least trying to land on the beach and in so doing would kill the lot of us. There was no sound. These things flew so fast the sound hadn't reached us yet, and as I stood staring at my last few moments on earth, I realised that it was one of the lads 'playing silly buggers' and had forgotten that Shamsan the mountain and 1700ft of rock stood between him and his maker.

At the last minute, with an almighty roar of its powerful engines the Valiant stood on its tail and tipping sharply to its left thankfully negotiated the rock wall - just.

We were deafened and all stood (or lay) in silence, frozen with fear. The aircraft had passed over us barely thirty feet from the sand. Someone picked our ball up, and we all made our way back to camp in virtual silence and in a state of shock. I don't wish to experience that moment again.

What with a dose of dysentery and a low flying, roaring Valiant it's a wonder it didn't give me a headache or two.

But thankfully my Migraines were gone forever.

BLOCK FIVE BOTTOM WEST

Within a couple of days of arriving in Aden and throwing my Kit bag on an M.T. bed, I had soon made friends with some of the lads around me who had all, of course, been in the Protectorate for some time and were looking brown and gnarled. They were not all M.T. lads by any means, as it turned out, and included a very serious intellectual bespectacled chap in his early twenties. He had finished his University course before being called up. He had a first in Chemistry, and he told me that he worked for I.C.I. He was a very introverted sort of a chap and kept himself very much to himself, but when he found out that my brother was an analytical chemist he did talk to me a little. He told me that he had discovered, quite by accident, whilst experimenting in the laboratory, a material for coating the inside of the barrels that they transport crude oil in.

"Blimey" I said, "You must be rich for discovering that. They must use that all over the world."

"Yes it is universally used now" he explained " But I didn't get paid for my discovery. As a researcher that's what the company pay me for. They did give me a welcome bonus however, and a promise of early promotion when I'm demobbed. So I am more than happy."

My immediate bedmate on my right hand was a super lad who came from Sheffield I believe, and who had a degree in Metallurgy. We spent many hours in deep conversation, talking about all kinds of things. In that respect he reminded me of my brother Colin who would discuss virtually anything (usually scientific) with me, and in their way were giving me the benefit of their education and wider knowledge of the world.

He spent his entire free time writing a book. It was a well-researched work and it was concerning the meaning of life. He told me, as he progressed with his study, that although he didn't have the answer he was looking for, he was convinced that by the time he completed the book he would find it. As he researched each religion in turn, and read various tomes written by some of the world's great philosophers and theologians (the RAF camp library was very accommodating and would get him most books that he requested) he would discuss their various ideas and apparent anomalies with me and ask for my view.

It was very stimulating for me, and although a lot of the lads regarded him as a bit odd, I can assure you he wasn't. Eventually he had produced hundreds of pages of closely hand written script, and he asked me if I could smuggle him into the Teleprinter room during the evenings when it was quiet, for him to type it up. Night after night, for weeks on end, he converted his book to type.

Sadly, when he had completed his work, and after he had let me read it, he inexplicably destroyed it. He was certain that he had found the 'answer' to why we were here and what life was all about. When he explained it to me, (and we argued long and hard about his findings), he eventually convinced me that maybe he was right.

Even to this day I would not like to say he was wrong.

All I will say is - I really hope he was.

Sadly, (and I am ashamed to admit this), although I slept alongside him for fourteen months, and even have a photograph of him, I have completely forgotten his name.

I haven't forgotten his remarkable book though or his conclusions to all of his research.

I can even remember the opening line of that book. A line that he pondered long and hard over as he was convinced it was that first sentence in any book that 'sold it'.

It was: -

'Theodore Maxim stared at the head of the man sitting in front of him…'

The story goes on to tell of Theodore tripping as he left the theological convention that he had been attending, and tumbling down the long flight of stone steps and knocking his head. He found himself being carried, in his hallucinatory dreams, on a long journey of enlightenment, visiting one by one, all the leaders of all the various religions of the world, from Jesus to Buddha to Mohammad, and asking each one of them just what it was that motivated them and their profound thoughts.

A fascinating book, and a great shame that my bedmate chose not to share it with the world.

Each block, I had noticed, had a small balcony tacked onto the end of the top floor, and occasionally one would see a very fit looking young man nip in and out (perhaps to collect his washing). No one seemed to take much interest in these 'phantoms', but just before I came home I heard tell that these brave young men were S.A.S., taking a well-earned rest from duties 'up country.'

Everyone in Aden had to find some interest to while away the hours of free time available, to stop them going bonkers. Many read of course, and a few studied. One of the lads in my billet took it upon himself to design and make a gadget that fitted on the front of his camera lens to enable him to take two entirely different shots on one piece of film. After many months of trying he eventually succeeded. I possess a picture of me admiring myself dressed as a young maiden, and it fools all but the most observant when they see it. He took photos of men playing chess with themselves, riding a bicycle with themselves on the handlebars, and goodness knows what else. It was a brilliant contraption, and must have been worth a fortune back in blighty. It certainly gave us all plenty to smile about.

Each billet had an Arab servant (bearer) and ours was a skinny little man by the name of Issam. He was about, I guess, thirty-five years old or so but he seemed much older. Each block had a bearer (self appointed) who was the 'Chai Walla' (senior man) and it was he who made the most money as the other bearers in that block had to buy their chai from him. The bearer was paid about three East African shillings per week per Erk, and for your money you were supplied with a mug of chai per day and your bed space was cleaned along with your shoes and kit. He also kept the ablutions clean and was the general odd job man. Getting a job as a bearer was much sought after, and Issam told me he had already saved enough to buy two wives who lived in his village up-country, and that he hoped to buy a couple more, plus some goats and a camel before he retired. I often wonder what happened to all those bearers when the British were driven out of Aden not many years later.

Issam (as did most Arabs) continually chewed a dark green leaf called 'Ghat.' I understand it was (amongst other things) an aphrodisiac. If it was, I often wondered why Issam chewed it, as he only visited his wives one week per year.

Issam nearly got my block knocked off about a week into my Aden life.

One afternoon, we were all lying on our pits copiously sweating when a loud bellow of "Issam" came from Big Steve's corner. The little man scurried the length of the billet to do the 'boss-man's' bidding to be greeted with a hefty cuff and a torrent of abuse for failing to do something trivial (I have forgotten what). I wasn't having that, and up off my bed, I strode naked down the billet (my bed was halfway down the room) to be confronted by a naked colossus.

"Cut that out big man" I said, "There's no need to hit him."

Issam cowered whimpering, coopied down against the wall.

"Off you go now and get Steve his chai" I said.

Everyone by now had rolled over on their pit and were waiting to watch Big Steve's challenger bite the dust.

By now I was already wishing that I had stayed put, but I was there, and my stupid pride was not going to allow me to stand down.

Remembering dad's words of long ago, I (coolly as I could) looked him straight in the eye. Those blue eyes were blazing, but I detected that very slight wavering that had been there on our first encounter.

"Go back to your bed space Moon-man, and if you still feel the same way this time next week I will take you out onto the balcony and hit sixteen bells out of you."

Relieved, deep inside, to be let off the hook, I simply said,

"We'll see big man, but don't let me see you hit him again."

And I skid-addled back to the sanctuary of my pit.

From that moment, I got my mug of chai last, my bed spaced was poorly cleaned, and very often my shoes were bypassed. When I politely asked Issam to 'buck up' he just looked at me with disdain.

A week after the incident I was (like everyone else) bellowing

"Issam - impshee you little Arab runt," - and service came back to normal.

I had only been in Aden a week and I had learned that Arabs take kindness as a weakness in men. They greatly respect strength and power.

Politicians of today would do well to understand this.

I walked down to Steve's bed (clothed this time) and offered my hand in apology. He accepted it warmly and we became good friends. Sadly, he was sent home some months later, to recover after catching some bug or other after taking a convoy of lorries up-country to Dhala. He was lucky to come out of it alive. Over two days we saw this giant of a man melt away before our very eyes. Whatever it was he had, the medics managed to save him, and he was sent home to the RAF hospital at Wroughton for specialised treatment. I am pleased to say that he made a full recovery, as he told us in his letters to his old M.T. mates left out in the sun.

Our little bed spaces quickly became your home, and very personal to you. There were no physical barriers, but each space, small as it was, was treated as your own little personal patch, and as such, that space was not violated unless you were invited by the owner of said patch, to sit on his bed. There were many times when I would seek the sanctuary of it to collect my thoughts. Many hours were spent lying on that bed (pit) pondering the meaning of life, and just why we were all put on this planet. I found answers to many of the so-called imponderables, but as for the question 'Why are we here?' I came to the conclusion (and I have never been convinced I was wrong about it) that we are here for one reason only.

SIMPLY TO RECREATE THE SPECIES.

Don't ask me to what end, because I don't know. But one thing is for sure, if everyone fails in this duty, everything that we know and believe in will have been for nothing at all.

Just ask Neanderthal Man.

That bed space consisted of a tall locker, a small bedside locker and of course your bed. Your bed had a mattress and a pillow and you were issued with two sheets and a pillowcase. It was so hot you slept with just the sheet covering your modesty, but even that covering proved too much, as in the night, in your sleep, often you would kick it off to try for a little respite from the sapping humidity. Should you be first to awake, it was a rare sight to gaze along the rows of beds and see your sleeping comrades all stood to attention, with the ever buzzing, voracious flies inspecting their equipment. Your bed linen was changed weekly when the Dhobi Walla came, and when he would take your shirts, socks, and shorts to be washed at the same time. I distinctly remember the starched khaki shirts that took a day's sweat to soften them up. Your underwear, handkerchiefs and civvie shirts and shorts etc. were done personally and hung out to dry outside your door (every bed space had it's own door out onto the balcony). The washing lines were rarely full as within ten minutes of hanging your gear out it was bone dry and ready for ironing. When not on duty all one would wear was flip-flops (no socks) and a pair of shorts. You didn't go out into the sun of course. If you needed to, you always made certain you were wearing a shirt.

Each Erk had displayed prominently on his locker door a 'chuff chart.' This simple (but crucial to ones sanity) chart, displayed the number of days left to demob. Religiously, every day that passed, a square would be filled in. As the blanks became fewer and fewer the excitement of seeing England and your loved ones again rose.

One of the bonuses of course, was the fact that you never got to complete your chart because you were usually sent home days before your two years were up.

In my case thirteen days, as I left Aden on 27th April 1958.

Although I have a photo showing my 'chuff chart' I regret not taking it down and keeping it as a keepsake. It certainly kept me perked up on many occasion.

That chart played a large part in my mental well being in that hot and arid land. Alongside your chuff chart one would display a picture of your sweetheart, and it was always a sad day when occasionally one of the lads received a 'Dear John', and the unfeeling young ladies photo' was replaced by a picture of Brigitte Bardot or Marilyn Monroe.

The pictures occasionally changed, but the 'chuff chart' always kept pride of place.

THAT LONGED FOR LETTER

Mail was crucial to the lads morale, and arrived sporadically. Sometimes we might have to wait as long as three weeks. But the day it arrived it was greeted with great excitement. The billet would descend into silence, as words were read and re-read. In my billet there was one lad who, in the whole of the fourteen months that I was there, did not receive one piece of mail. No birthday card - not even a Christmas card. Now, whether he ever wrote home to his family I know not. He said he did, but it was very sad. We all took it in turns to read him one of ours. For me, I was lucky. I always had loads of regular letters (most of which I still have) The one I looked forward to most of all was the special one from my pretty Persian Princess, which almost always consisted of a one page Airmail letter, but smothered in lipstick kisses.

I was the envy of the billet.

Sister Pam wrote every week without fail, supplying me with all the family news and a list of all the latest jokes taken from the radio. Once a week, Gordon Thomas, my old cricketing opening partner at Hambrook, sat down after lunch on a Sunday, and kept me up to date with the village news. Gordon had promised me that he would write every week. He told me that when he was in the Army, in Egypt doing his National Service, he rarely got a letter, and knew just how important a few lines from home could be.

To see a pile (or even one letter) of mail all addressed to: -

    5019897 AC NORTHAM
    BLOCK 5 Bottom West
    RAF KHORMAKSAR
    B.F.P.O. 69

Certainly lifted the spirits. And I would say without doubt, that 'Mail Day' was the most important day of your service life.

At Christmas, sister Pam baked me one of her magnificent Christmas cakes, and sent it with other goodies to cheer me up. Fred her husband, who had served both in the North African desert and Italy during the war, had elaborately iced the cake, forgetting just how hot the desert could be; and when I opened the parcel, and with all the lads gathered around me awaiting their slice - as I had forewarned them that my sister's wonderful cake was on the way -

they saw the gooey mess staring up at them and turned away. Only the hungriest stayed as I sank my knife into the delicious interior.

That cake did not last 10 minutes as back they came for more. I did (perhaps greedily) hide an extra big 2nd piece for me to consume later in secret.

The lads agreed as one, that Pam's cake was by far the best that the billet had received. There was a sequel, however. My 20th Birthday was on January 26th and as it so happened the mail was late arriving, and we didn't get it until around 10th February. To be honest I had completely forgotten my birthday and it had come and gone without me knowing. It was only when I got back to the billet from a late shift that I saw my pile of mail on my bed, and an opened parcel with a half eaten cake inside.

Unforgivable! One's mail was sacrosanct. Not to be touched under any circumstances. The lads gathered around my bed like a bunch of shamed children saying.

"We knew there was one of your sister's cakes in there and we just could not wait for you to get back."

What could I say? At least they left me half of it to enjoy.

Which I did with relish.

When I arrived in Aden I was told that I had just missed payday, and that I would have to wait two weeks until the next one. I was skint and I knew no one. Luckily I had found the equivalent of about 4/- in East African money that fellow villager John Bracey had given me the day before I left home. John had served in Aden for a short while, and indeed had been stationed at Khormaksar as a storeman. He had been sent home early with a really bad case of 'Aden Ear'. John had found this bit of loose change in his belongings and kindly handed it over saying,

"It's no use to me and it will buy you a weeks supply of fags when you get out there." What a Godsend.

Cigarettes were ridiculously cheap in Aden, it being a duty free port. And you could buy twenty Senior Service for about the equivalent of nine pence (4 1/2p in current money). The virtually free ciggies were to a degree my downfall as, (like a lot of other fools around me) I smoked much too much, and that dreaded addictive drug Nicotine got hold of me. Not only did it ruin my health and restrict my sporting activities; I once worked it out that up until the time I gave it up, at around thirty-one years of age, the money I had wasted on it could have bought me two houses.

To this day it is one of the only two regrets that I have in life. I cannot believe that I was fool enough to have ever smoked. The other, for the record, is that I did not get myself properly educated - I had the chance, and I threw that away.

Anyway, there I was, 5000 miles from home and stoney broke.

I immediately wrote a begging letter home to Parvin asking for a loan. Not knowing the state of the postal service at the time, I was not surprised to receive, two days before payday, a lipstick smothered letter containing a brand new 10/- note.

That 10/- saved my life. Come to think of it I never paid her back. (Or John for that matter).

Talking of mail and its influences.

Some time about mid-way through my tour, three or four of the lads from another billet dressed up in sheets, exposing only their eyes and had a photograph taken, sending it to The Reveille or some such weekly 'fun' paper, with an accompanying letter stating that there were no girls in Aden, (which there weren't) and that all the lads had to look at were in the enclosed picture. The newspaper printed the photo and letter, and the very next post the boys received eight or ten sacks of mail containing thousands letters from young ladies from all over the U.K.

Some of the letters were very amorous indeed, and a few contained some very alluring photographs. Some even contained underwear.

What a wonderful bunch the British girls are. They really did want to make their 'soldier boys' stay away from home a little more comforting.

They tell me that all the letters were answered (although I didn't volunteer as I had more than my share of letters to write each week), and many friendships established.

I often wonder if anything came of those pen pals.

A GAMBLING ERROR

Our Dhobi Walla ('Abdul the Shirt') had a brother called Omar who was a bit of an entrepreneur. Every Sunday morning he would arrive with his suitcase containing everything from shirts to toothbrushes. He did a roaring trade as his stuff was good quality, and he was cheaper than the NAAFI. He was a genial character and I liked him. For one thing he possessed an English sense of humour, and never minded a joke against himself or the Arabs in general, and he was not short of a quick quip or clever bit of repartee either.

Our Sunday mornings at that time, had become for an hour or so, a nine card brag gambling 'school.' Four of us had got together and used my bed as a table. We enjoyed throwing our East African copper coins into a pile in the centre of the bed, where we had an old sheet laid out to catch the loot, in the vain hope it would be our turn to 'cop' the kitty and walk away with a few pounds bonus for the week.

Stupid game nine-card brag, but the lads enjoyed it and it passed an hour. If (as was usual) the pot wasn't won when the hour was up, we would wrap up the money in the sheet, stow it in my locker, and continue the game the following Sunday. Omar, after he had finished his trading, would often stand watching, until one day (after a reasonable sized 'pot' had been won) he asked if he could have a game.

He had been fascinated by our raucous cheers and micky taking, and wanted to join in.

"No way Abdul" my card playing mates said, "Go and sell your shirts like a good little A-rab."

Disappointed, Omar persisted week after week with his request, until eventually the boys agreed to let him play.

"I don't think so boys" I said, "What if he wins the 'pot' and it's a big'un. We wont like it."

"Na, he'll be alright" they said, "He won't know how to play properly anyway."

With winks all round Omar took his seat.

He joined in readily, but now with one extra in the school the odds against getting three winning hands to win the booty became almost astronomical.

Right from the start this proved to be so, and often it was Omar who thwarted an eager 'winner.'

Three or four weeks went by and now there must have been £30 sitting there.

£30 was a fortune to an impoverished Irkie, and the tension mounted.

I could see in a couple of my pals eyes that 'gleam of gold' that reminded me of words that Robert Louis Stevenson had written describing the cut-throat mates of Long John Silver in Treasure Island. These men were being turned by the sight of money - a large amount of money.

You guessed it - Omar won it.

Believe it or not, with two prials and an ace flush. Blimey he deserved to win it with a hand like that.

As he gleefully reached for the pot my three colleagues rose as one.

"On your way Abdul - the money's ours."

"Come on lads" I exclaimed "He won it fair and square," and I quickly bundled up the sheet and pile of loot, handed it to Omar and said,

"Get on out of it matey boy - and fast."

In a flash he was gone with his swag flung over his shoulder and his suitcase in his other hand. I turned to face my angry mates. Much venom was spit in my direction but nought else.

It was the last game of nine-card brag that we played, and it was the last we saw of Omar, which was a pity because our mobile shop had been a great convenience. That jovial Arab probably bought himself another wife with his winnings from his first foray into the world of brag, whilst the NAAFI's profits increased.

To placate the lads I encouraged them to turn to Monopoly.

Others in the billet joined us, and we used our Sunday mornings competing in an improvised 'Aden Monopoly League', which in the end proved to be lots more fun, and was much better than the card game.

We played four-handed, alternating the make up of the four so that we all played against one another an equal number of times. We dealt out the cards, and spent a fixed ten minutes bartering with one another to acquire sets, before playing for a set 90 minutes after which time was called. The person with the largest assets at that point scored 10 points, second highest scored 5 points, third 3 points and fourth 2 points.

I am pleased to report that I was the undefeated Aden Monopoly champion and the lads were glad to see me demobbed.

The reason for my success at this best of all board games was (allied to a bit of luck with the dice of course) purely observation of how the game was laid out.

Although the man who devised the game had got the prices and money pretty much right, I had noticed a slight flaw in how the game was set up and how, given reasonable luck of the dice, the odds could be worked in your favour, and I milked it for all it was worth. Nobody else noticed what I was doing and just called me 'a jammy git.'

'Jammy git' or not, I ended up Aden Monopoly champion every time.

FALLING IN LOVE

Six months into my Aden life a remarkable thing happened.

Apart from the fact that, as dad had predicted, I had not had one single headache - funnily enough a fact that I barely took too much notice of at the time. I suppose you only notice a headache when you have a headache, and when you are free of it you just get on with life - I suddenly realised that in my contemplative moments and dreaming of home - instead of thinking of mother, I found that I was mostly thinking of Parvin. When I examined my thoughts closely, I came to realise that I had fallen in love - and we were five thousand miles apart.

Nineteen years of age and Cupids arrow had at last found its mark.

THE LAND OF BUGS

Once a month the 'Bug Walla' paid us a visit. He turned up with his brass canister strapped to his back and proceeded to spray the underside of our beds, with some obnoxious smelling spray.

I couldn't stand that smell, and the bugs certainly didn't enjoy it either.

The first time that I saw those bugs dropping, literally, in their hundreds from under my bed, made me feel queasy. From that day on I had to get used to the thought that I slept with others. Thank God they didn't snore or for that matter fancy taking a bite to eat under cover of darkness.

Those little varmints weren't the only wildlife around.

Apart from the flies that I have already described, there were hundreds of Kites (known as 'Shite Hawks' to the lads) which were forever wheeling around in the thermals overhead. They had been known to swoop and clear your plate at the mess before you could sit down, if you were foolish enough to take your food and sit outside the dining hall on the shaded balcony in an effort to try and keep cool.

Those Kites enjoyed the cookhouse grub if no one else did.

Luckily they didn't bother me as for 50% of the time my food was collected and eaten before the mess actually opened. We had a special dispensation as we worked shifts. We were either first in or one of the last to eat. Either way it didn't improve the grub, but it meant we could nearly always get a spot under a fan. The food was awful, but I didn't blame the cooks, they had the worst job on the camp.

Occasionally you would catch a glimpse of an enormous hairy spider, some as big as your hand. But they didn't care for humans much, and if disturbed would scurry away like lightning. There was a load of them in and around the Airmans Club. The first time that I saw one I thought it was a rat, but apparently they were harmless enough. I remember once seeing a young Arab bearer chasing one of these giants around and around the Airman's club wielding a tin tray as a weapon, and every abortive crash of the tray winning a loud roar from the watching Erkies. I don't remember him catching the poor old hairy monster after all of his efforts, which was just as well as it would have been a shame to put to death such a beautiful creature.

From time to time the Arab bearer would appear with a couple of Praying Mantis and flog them to any pet lover. For a while I owned one, and it lived happily (or seemingly happily) on the top of my small locker. I had secured him with a piece of cotton around his spindly leg, and I made him a little house out of a small cardboard box. I used to catch him flies and bring him in the odd bit of greenery if any could be found. He was about 5 or 6 inches tall and bright green in colour. His head reminded me of The Mekon of Dan Dare and The Eagle fame. Poor sod met his end when the twat of a Bug Man turned up unannounced one day and gave him a squirt from his brass canister.

I gave him a proper burial just outside the billet door - but I never got another.

Once, the entire camp was invaded by a swarm of bright green Locusts. Goodness knows what they were doing in Aden, as there was absolutely nothing for them to eat. I must admit there wasn't millions of the hated monsters as subsequently seen on television when they invade the Serengeti, although the air was quite thick with them for a while as they buzzed around and around in a hapless and fruitless search for food, and I suppose there must have been tens of thousands in total. They didn't hang about long and were only with us for about a day. Their visit intrigued me however, and catching one, I had a chance to study the creature close at hand. It was no more than a giant Grasshopper as I saw it. Quite an ugly brute really and would have been pretty scary if it grew a little bit more.

The evening prior to the swarm's visit, The Pentagons were performing at the Families Club, and whilst Rod and I were on stage, one of these flying monsters flew through the footlights and landed on my chest. What followed (obviously quite unrehearsed) was as funny a piece of comedy that I have witnessed. Rod 'milked' that incident for ten minutes or more before the creature realised there were tastier things around other than my white shirt. Roderick was a very funny man and used this totally unexpected occurrence to drain the audience dry of laughter. I have often thought what a pity those moments could not have been recorded.

But they came and went, never to be repeated ever again.

Many years later I was helping Pete Woore (who worked for Rentokil at the time) fumigate a large cargo ship in Cardiff docks, when I found one lone Locust hiding amongst the bananas. I put the green monster in a small box that one of the Greek seamen found for me, brought it home, and the next evening when all the lads were gathered at cricket practice on the Common, secretly released it on to the cricket square. It frightened everyone to death as I said (pointing at our enormous green friend)

"Look at the size of that Grasshopper?"

One of my fellow Erkies great pastimes (pleasures?) which I must confess I did not share, was when, from time to time, someone would catch a Scorpion. Immediately the cry would go up "Scorpion - Scorpion" and in no time a crowd would gather out on the balcony to watch it put to death.

They would spray a half circle of lighter fuel in the corner, put the poor old Scorpion inside and set light to the fuel. The Scorpion would run around and around looking for safety, and when it realised there was no way out, its sting would flick over it's back and sting itself behind its head.

Bloody cruel I thought, and utterly pointless when a well-aimed heel could have dispatched the creature swiftly. I know the little blighters could do you no good if they crawled into your shoes during the night, but I must admit after witnessing my first cruel execution I didn't want to see another. Incidentally, I never once heard of anyone ever having been stung by one of these greatly maligned and rather attractive creatures.

Packs of wild dogs (Pyards) lived on the little islands in the harbour and twice a year a party of crack shots were sent out from the camp to cull them. Although you would see them roaming about in their packs from time to time, and they did look a scrawny flea ridden bunch of curs, I couldn't see what harm they were doing, but then I wasn't exactly concentrating on the problem (if there was one).

The main animal in Aden was of course the Camel. The Arabs used them as pack animals, they milked them and they ate them. I dread to think how much Camel meat I must have ate during my fourteen months in that God forsaken land, and if I did, I could not tell you what it tasted like. Camels, although domesticated, were private kind of animals and definitely had a mind of their own. When they were resting and eating they were not too disposed to being disturbed.

One day when we were walking through the narrow streets of Maala we came upon a resting camel train who were quietly sitting in a group chewing the cud, and no doubt contemplating their heavy burdens and the long walk back to Sheik Othman during the coming night. Taff Nash, in his friendly Welsh manner, decided to smooth a rather handsome looking specimen sitting at the head of the pack. As he rubbed his nose and said hello, the camel turned his head and spat a full half a pint of foul smelling green liquid straight into Taff's face, and as the shocked Welshman staggered back the laconic camel continued to chew on his dinner, lost in his own thoughts.

Second to the Camel in number, was the goat. The locals kept many of these, and like the Camel they milked them, and ate them. I do remember enjoying a goat steak in a restaurant in Crater City on one of the only couple of times I visited the place. It wasn't unpleasant but I could not describe the taste now, so it could not have been too memorable.

The main indigenous creature of Aden was without doubt the dreaded fly. There were literally trillions of them and some of them were aggressive little (or big) varmints. Their main place of abode was the latrines at the transit camp and the Mess. Old sweats would love to tease the Moonmen on early arrival in Khormaksar with the warning to 'watch out for the shit-fly'. This mythical fly was said to gorge itself at the open latrines until it could barely fly, before struggling into the air, gaining a little height and making for anyone that moved, before smashing into them like some Kamikaze pilot and committing suicide as it exploded and sprayed the target with well chewed crap. One could always pick out a Moonman as he walked tentatively about his business looking permanently to the sky.

They say that God put all creatures on this earth with a purpose, but apart from making a tasty meal for my Praying Mantis, I can't for the life of me explain what they were doing in Aden.

NOT SO FRIENDLY ARABS

By and large most of the Arabs were friendly and appreciated the money being brought into the Protectorate by the Services, but there were a number (rightly I suppose) who objected to our presence, and wanted us out. I reckoned most of those 'English haters' lived in Crater, and so I didn't like going there, but my mates thought I was being over cautious.

I didn't like Crater - I didn't feel safe.

Aden was a duty free port, and so Passenger Liners on the way to or from Australia and the Far East would call in from time to time, and the travellers would spend their money on the cheap watches - cameras - gold and silver jewellery and perfume. No doubt this still occurs and brings welcome cash to the area, but when the time came for the British to leave it must have left a large hole in their economy.

Back to Crater.

One day half a dozen of us were making our way in Indian file, down a very narrow street where the mud brick houses were about three stories high, when I happened to glimpse a slight movement from one of the roofs. Luckily I was at the back of our column and was able to shout a warning just as an Arab threw a very large chunk of masonry at the lad in the front, who fortunately heeded my call of "Get back," and the missile, as big as a man's head, shattered into a million fragments not two feet in front him. We yelled of course, but our assailant, having failed in his dastardly deed, was across the rooftops and long gone before we could do anything.

My other vivid memory of Crater was much more pleasant. I had heard tell of the historic Sheba Tanks that were located close to the town, and we went to visit them. These water tanks were thousands of years old, and legend had it that they were commissioned by the great Queen of Sheba herself, whose Kingdom reached down from the Yemen interior to the Indian Ocean at Aden. They were built to ensure a plentiful supply of drinking water for her subjects.

These tanks were enormous reservoirs held in naturally formed underground caves in the centre of the long extinct volcano from whence Crater took its name. My memory of those tanks was of vast caverns filled to the brim with cool clear water that (presumably) were replenished from the condensation that must have formed high on the slopes of Shamsan during the night, and somehow trickled down to be collected in these natural caverns. That water couldn't have come from rain because it never rained. Well it did, twice in my time, so they might just have been able to catch enough. Those caves (water tanks) were quite a wonder to me at the time, and I would have liked to have had a little more time to explore the history of them.

Shamsan, the mountain that overlooked the harbour and Steamer Point, was 1700ft high and local legend had it that if you climbed her you would one day return. I did climb her once, along with a few of my mates, but foolishly tackled it from the Steamer Point side. Although it wasn't a difficult ascent, the fact that we were in shorts, and would you believe, wearing flip-flops and carrying no water, put the degree of difficulty up 200%. We made it though, although I can't prove it because, foolishly, none of us had a camera with us. On reaching the summit (where it was ever so slightly cooler) we were somewhat surprised to find a donkey track running down the other side all the way into Crater. This track, naturally, we availed ourselves of on the descent, and I can distinctly remember sitting in the shade outside the first Arab tea shop we reached, quaffing pints of ice cold Coke to replenish the liquid lost on the way up.

I don't suppose now that I will ever return to Aden so that part of the legend is lost.

Dry and arid Aden may have been, but the Queen of Sheba ingeniously solved the drinking water problem thousands of years ago with her spectacular caverns.

Not for us the natural way: The canny British solved their water problem in an entirely different manner.

Our billets had three or four large headed showers that were in constant use as you might imagine, as it was here that you were able to get a little respite from the unbearable humidity.

Surprisingly perhaps for the desert, there was unlimited water (all cold I might add). Well it wasn't cold, more tepid really, as it was stored in two enormous water tanks that stood on stilts in the blazing sun, on the edge of the camp. I am not sure, but I think there must have been a desalination plant somewhere close by, but in truth that was something I never queried. Certainly the water from the taps was only just drinkable, and had a peculiar taste. It was not salty as such, but because it was lukewarm it was pretty much unpalatable. They used to supply copious amounts of Lemon and or Orange crystals to give it a bit of taste. It helped, but was very acidic, and you had to be careful that you didn't use too much at a time or you would find you were soon peeing tintacks.

One downside to the tepid water was that you had to shave in it. You soon got used to it however, and quickly learned that to perform your daily task in comfort, you simply used a little more shaving soap and lathered up for twice as long as normal.

This was OK, but on one occasion I definitely slipped up.

We had just seen a marvellous film called 'The Vikings' starring Kirk Douglas and Tony Curtis, and as I thought Tony Curtis looked rather fetching in his beard, and I was in one of my 'no need to work' periods at the time, I decided to try to grow one. It didn't look too bad (I thought) although in that stifling heat it was not a very good idea really, and so after a week or ten days it had to come off. That was the most agonising shave that I ever experienced (apart from the half a dozen efforts during my Jankers at Hednesford, when I was cruelly victimised by a sadistic officer).

Cold water, dodgy razor blade and half grown beard. Not recommended. Sadly I didn't have a picture taken of that 'Viking beard' before it disappeared forever.

Shan't do that again.

Those showers, however, were a godsend when on the three or four occasions a sandstorm blew in. The choking dust could be avoided by standing beneath the cascading water, and everyone made a dive for them and a bit of relief from the cloud from hell. A photo of twenty or so naked youths all clustered together in the showers seeking sanctuary would have made a good centre spread for Time Magazine. I found it better (and more comfortable) to soak a towel in water and lie on my bed with it covering my head and with it tucked in around the sides. Eventually most of the lads copied me, and reckoned I should have patented the idea. Why no one hadn't thought of it before I know not. It wasn't totally fool proof however, because in that terrible heat your towel would dry out regularly, and you had to 'wet-up' again. One of those sandstorms hung about for almost two days, but normally they came and went in twelve hours or so. I have a remarkable picture taken from Block 5 roof just minutes before a sandstorm struck.

THE ASTRA

The camp open-air cinema, The Astra, played a big part in my life in Aden.

Apart from the scene of my performances in the Big Variety Show that took place after I had only been in the desert for just a matter of weeks, and the ENSA shows that came out to entertain us: we went to the pictures there four times every week.

The films were changed every two days, with the Sunday show a 'one dayer.' From memory it used to cost 5 East African cents (about a shilling in our money - 5p in decimal) to attend.

I can't really remember for sure, but I think it cost 10 cents to sit upstairs and these seats were usually full of Officers and their wives.

It was much more fun downstairs anyway.

All the latest films were shown, along with a fairly up to date Pathe Newsreel. We enjoyed the uncensored versions of the latest French films, which usually contained a bit of girlie flesh. These films were very popular with the lads as you might imagine, and with a young nubile Brigitte Bardot a particular favourite. The French films always seemed a little more risqué than ours, and for a female starved bunch of young bucks these celluloid fantasies helped pass the dreary months.

Although of course I enjoyed those films like every one else, my favourites, by miles, were the Westerns. There seemed to be plenty of them made in those days, unlike today, and stars like John Wayne and Richard Widmark became our great heroes. We would leave the cinema with our imaginary 'guns' slung low, and walk slowly back to the billet with our equally imaginary 'spurs' jangling. Occasionally a 'gun fight' would ensue. We all thought that we were 'the fastest gun alive' and despite many hectic battles, no one bit the dust.

To this day I can still quote some of the memorable lines from some of those marvellous movies.

About three weeks before I went home, one of the lads in my billet produced a pair of realistic looking reproduction Colt 45's and a gun belt (Goodness knows were he got them from). They were quite heavy, as the real thing must have been, and when they were slung around your waist you really did feel like a gun fighter. Did we have fun as, in turn, we buckled them on and tried to show our 'skills' at being 'quick on the draw.' I came to the conclusion that if I had lived in those Wild West days I would not have made old bones.

After Westerns, Musicals came next in popularity. Occasionally we would go to the second night performance of these films as well, especially if there were lots of pretty dancing girls on show. We quickly learned the popular songs and Rod would invariably 'lift' an idea to use in our cabaret performances.

Popular as the Westerns and Musicals were, most films shown were excellent entertainment and the stars of the day became 'good friends.' Somewhere I have a single frame of celluloid, (cut from the original reel of film by my pal who was the camp projectionist), of that classic moment from that wonderful film "The Seven Year Itch" featuring Marilyn Monroe with her skirt blowing up over her head as the train went by below, as she stood over the Sub-way grating.

My very first attendance of The Astra produced a big shock.

The show would always open with a couple of adverts. They were always the same, and included an advert for Lux Toilet soap starring that very pretty actress Kay Kendall who posed seductively in her negligee before taking a sumptuous bubble bath, whilst the commanding voice of Dickie Valentine urged us to study,

'The new star that had entered the firmament' as he sang: -

"Introducing Miss Kay Kendall
Her appeal is fundamental
And her advice to you
If you are longing to
Keep your skin like satin.
Is - when you choose
The soap to use
Be quite sure
It's white and pure.
It's used by nine out of every ten
Film stars - I mean girls not men.
You know the name it's
LUX - LUX - LUX
LUX TOILET SOAP.

Every one in the auditorium sang that song lustily, and, like their Service numbers, I bet they will never forget those words till the day they die - or Kay Kendall for that matter.

But it wasn't Miss Kendall that shocked me.

Immediately after the adverts they would show the Pathe Newsreel and following that, a short film of Her Majesty at the trooping of the colour, whilst they played the National Anthem. We all stood to attention of course, but I was horrified to hear most of my fellow members of the audience standing in the dark, letting out wolf whistles etc. when close ups of the Queen were shown. They did it every night and most thought it funny. I thought it pretty disgusting - and still do. I hope that I have a good sense of humour, and yes, there are some funny jokes made of our Royal Family that I can really laugh at, but doing this whilst your own National Anthem is being played? This really did not happen in 1957. We were British for god sake and should have been proud of it.

I can see now that this was probably the beginning of football yobbery, and the disrespect shown for the Anthems of other countries at sporting occasions that occurs in these 'modern' days. Perhaps if they had closed the Astra down for a week or so as punishment it would have nipped it in the bud.

Watching those films, particularly the musicals, gave us lots of ideas for our cabaret act, and when I wrote a Pantomime (which we performed on the new Airman's Club stage) it was loosely adapted from a marvellous film starring Danny Kaye called 'The Court Jester.'

We performed that Panto (called Boris in the Woods) twice only. The first performance was an afternoon matinee for all the women and kids in Aden and the second night an adult version for the lads. Both were highly acclaimed and we were disappointed that the powers that be did not allow us to take it around the Protectorate. But then, there was a war on I suppose.

When ENSA brought their shows out to entertain us we were lucky enough to be asked to stage-manage them. We met such stars as Harry Secombe, Eric Sykes and Billy Burden. All of these people were very friendly, and shared their time back stage with us, with great generosity.

I particularly remember Harry Secombe standing next to me in the wings suffering racks of stomach pain with the onset (probably) of Dysentery, before bounding out onto the stage to do his act, full of the joys of life. No one in that audience could have known how ill he was.

What a trooper.

Billy Burden, on finding out that I was a comic, and after I had asked him for words of advice should I take up the stage as a career, told me,

"Anyone can get a laugh with a blue joke son. To prove to yourself that you are funny - keep it clean."

I have long since discovered that he was right, but I must confess some of the funniest jokes I know are blue.

That aside, the Astra was a godsend to us Erkies, stranded out in the desert thousands of miles from home. It allowed us to be carried away, in our imaginations, to all parts of the world, before bringing us back to the reality of service life. I often wonder just how miserable life would have been without our beloved cinema.

THE AIRMANS CLUB

The Airman's Club was simply a bar and collection of quiet rooms surrounding a Terrazzoed square laid down originally as a dancing area I suppose. This area was about fifteen yards square and had a two-foot high 30ftx20ft uncovered and bare wooden dais alongside it (presumably to house a band should there be a dance). For all the time that I was out there I don't recall seeing anyone dance on that Terrazzo square. Mind you there were no women to dance with. It was here that we built a proper stage and dressing rooms, converting that two-foot high dais into a fair place of theatre. I have to put my hands up and say that I did little of the actual building. It was simply my idea that we should construct a proper stage, and I was able to help with the design and keep the whole project on track. I must say I was very pleased with our efforts, which I hope were improved upon when I left. There were some very skilled lads on camp, very eager to take on the project, and it was all done on a shoestring budget. Most of the materials used were acquired after going 'walkabout' from the various storerooms on camp. Our footlights for example should have adorned the edge of Khormaksar runway, and the curtains came from a very large bolt of cloth that had been earmarked for the NAAFI.

From memory we were given no financial assistance from the hierarchy, although they conveniently turned a blind eye to the pilfering of timber etc. that went on to complete the structure. The walls of the bar area in the club were adorned with some excellent paintings (usually of pretty girls), and the furniture was pretty spartan. Although it was used pretty extensively, most of the lads frequented the NAAFI in preference, but that was only because it had a couple of older ladies serving behind the bar. As I have said, females of any age were in very short supply in the desert. Mostly my pals and me loyally used the club, as it was here that we rehearsed our shows. There was rarely any trouble with drink in the club, although I do remember once a young lad on his 'Boat Party' (the celebratory booze up before you go home) getting exceedingly drunk after drinking a whole bottle of Rum in one go. He collapsed of course and was rushed to hospital. Apparently he almost died from alcoholic poisoning, and as well as missing his ticket home.

To make matters worse, he was put on a 'fizzer' for not looking after his own health. The whole camp was in shock for a few days and I don't think that stupidity ever occurred again.

Goodness knows how they came to get hold of it, but the Airmans Club owned three canisters of 32mm film containing the 1938 Olympic Games. From time to time these would be got out and played to (usually a full house in the club) a very enthusiastic audience who, at the start of each race would yell out with the sound track "Verteck" as the athletes prepared to race. Old Jessie Owens just didn't know how proud we were of him as he flashed down the track to win the 100 metres every time we saw it. I still remember the sickly smile on the face of Adolf Hitler as he crossed the line. Those cans of film would be worth a fortune now as, (as I understand it), they were filmed by that very famous German lady film producer Leni Riefenstahl, who pioneered the use of artistic close ups in the cinema.

They certainly brought us lads a great deal of pleasure I can tell you.

OPERATIONAL KHORMAKSAR

RAF Khormaksar was an operational station and boasted a first class runway which was shared with commercial traffic. Whilst I was there we flew Valiant Bombers and Venom fighters as our strike planes with Valettas and Beverley Transporters doing the bulk of the freighting.

As there was continual fighting 'up-country', the boys were in the air most days flying various sorties. The Black Watch (in my time) were being continually shipped up country to keep things in check, and barely a week went by without a life being lost. It was a war of sorts, but no one back home realised it. In that hot and desolate spot, however, lying in a barren but well cared for cemetery called Silent Valley, are the remains of almost five hundred brave young men: monument to the struggle that went on virtually unknown to the rest of England.

There were some spectacular near misses in amongst the tragedies. One lad, when his brakes failed him, overshot the runway and ploughed onto the beach. The nose of his Venom was ripped off and he was left with absolutely nothing in front of him except fresh air. All he got for his trouble was a badly gashed cheek. Another lad was the centre of three flying down a valley with mountains either side, when they ran into a hail of tribesmen's 505 Calibre rifle fire. Struck by one of these 'mini-shells' his kite burst into flames and crashed into the side of a mountain, but not before he miraculously ejected seconds before it struck. Luckily for him the Black Watch were in the near vicinity and they found him sitting on a rock nursing a broken leg.

Tales were told (I don't know how true they were) of the odd serviceman being taken prisoner by the tribesmen, handed over to the women folk who slit their throats, sewed their testicles to their lips, before leaving them out in the cruel sun to act as decoys to ensnare the rescue party.

Aden in 1957/58 was a lively spot to be. For my part, me and my mates had a narrow escape when the Beverley that was to take us up-country during a leave break - particularly to see the Turtles on Bahrain Island - crashed whilst landing at Dhala (about 80 miles from Khormaksar) killing two of the crew.

Apparently the airfield at Dhala was located in a narrow valley, and just as the aircraft was about to touch down a freak gust of wind blew it marginally off of the tarmac and it somersaulted into the sand. The tail section, in which we would have been sitting, was smashed to smithereens.

We got to see most photographs of such calamities, as being in signals these were passed through the office, and when we saw what was left of our plane it was a very sobering sight.

That fateful trip had already been postponed two or three times before. This time we were actually on the tarmac, and walking toward the aircraft, when we were sent back and told that the plane would be overloaded with us on board, as they had needed to load extra ammunition to quell another uprising.

We never did get to see the Turtles, or anywhere else up-country for that matter, but at least we were in one piece.

Looking back to that fateful day I still can't believe my luck and the ill luck of Flight Lieutenant Drummond and his brave men, and the fact that a mere gust of wind at the wrong moment could have left my soul in the dusty sands of Dhala.

Although I am still not terribly fond of flying - I prefer to keep my feet on the ground - being part of a very busy operational RAF station, and being able to sit on top of the Signals block alongside the runway during my breaks and watch the lads buzz in and out in a seemingly never ending stream, gave me a love and interest in aircraft that has never left me.

SHEIK OTHMAN

The farthest North I got was the little Oasis town of Sheik Othman fifteen or twenty miles up country from Khormaksar. It was quite an experience and I am glad I went, although my biggest memory of that trip was stopping by a small muddy pool of water, miles from anywhere and right in the middle of the desert. How did it get there? I never found the answer. We spent but little time in the township of Sheik Othman itself, before we were taken by our taxi driver to the Oasis that gave birth to its existence. This magical spot was amazingly lush and green, with date palms and exotic flowering bushes in abundance. Most of all there was grass growing there. It wasn't an enormous area. From memory I doubt if it covered an acre and had been turned into a sort of park. We spent a most pleasant couple of hours there away from the dust and sand.

That day we had hired a taxi to drive us, but on the only other occasion that I visited the town our transport was far different.

The 'Snowdrops' had become good friends of ours, as they often used to call into the signals block during the night for a cuppa chai and perhaps a 'listen in' on the telephone extension. Many times they invited us to go with them on 'the brothel run' to Sheik Othman to have a look around. They had told us many funny stories of their adventures, and eventually I was persuaded to join Rod and a very new, gleaming white, baby faced addition, to our now burgeoning Signal staff, who had been in Aden but a week, no more, on one of these runs.

It was strictly against the RAF rules for the lads to frequent these Arab houses of ill repute, as anyone who did would invariably bring back more than they bargained for, and the Snowdrops would do regular raids ('spot' checks as they would put it) to deter the rest of the troops, so this was an opportunity for us to see this sordid side of life legally.

It was an experience I wont forget but must say would not want to repeat.

On arriving in Sheik Othman in total darkness (no moon that night and there was no such thing as street lights), we pulled up in our jeep outside the first of these mud built houses. We entered the dingy oil lamp lit building in single file led by our Snowdrop friends.

I was bringing up the rear.

The Snowdrops who, although they hadn't drawn their pistols had unbuttoned the holster in readiness, had whispered to us to keep alert and our eyes peeled.

Brushing through the dangling beaded 'door' we were greeted, firstly, with an almost overpowering smell of cheap perfume, before we entered this surprisingly large room seemingly packed with very pretty, very young, Arab girls. Each girl was lying on her own small bunk bed. As soon as we entered they, as one, raised their naked bodies onto an elbow and cried,

"Come on Johnny have me." offering their undoubted charms.

I must confess, mesmerised as I was, even if I had not been chaperoned by the Snowdrops, I couldn't have taken advantage of the display on offer.

I was frightened to death, particularly as seated at the back of the room were two villainous looking Arabs each wearing a lethal looking curved Jambiya dagger at the waist. They did not move however, and said nothing. If I was frightened, so was our little 'Moonman' friend, fresh out of England, when this pretty little Arab girl caught sight of his lily white skin she said slyly,

"Come on Chico - for you baksheesh."

He almost leapt into my arms with fear.

All the other houses we entered were filled in the same manner, and although I estimate we must have seen fifty or more girls, I did not witness one customer. Perhaps they had been forewarned of our coming.

I must say I couldn't get out of there fast enough and was very glad to see the lights of Khormaksar and the safety of my own little bed space.

Whist on the subject of ladies of the night, I was told that it was a thriving business in the Protectorate. One lad I knew would boast of the beautiful Italian lady who 'lived' in a hotel (there weren't too many hotels as I recall) in Steamer Point, and he would regularly visit her and stay the night for the princely sum of £20 (a fortune to a lowly paid airman) When asked where he got the money from, he used to smile and say,

'Daddy sends it from Blighty to help out with expenses.'

MISSING MOMBASA

Although Aden was hot and uncomfortable the RAF kindly supplied a leave camp in Mombasa - Kenya to give the lads a couple of weeks relief from the barren desert. Provided you gave plenty of notice they would fly you down for a fortnights leave, and you would stay in a specially set up leave camp there. All this luxury, which included trips to Nairobi and a Safari park, was yours for the princely sum of thirty pounds.

Sadly, and certainly in retrospect, foolishly, I did not avail myself of this chance of a lifetime, and spent my bit of savings on presents for the family. The lads who did go had a marvellous time and told of their trip to Nairobi, and climbing Kilimanjaro. They told of going on a three day Safari and seeing all the wild life up close. To think I could have done all of that for less than £30. It would cost thousands now.

Bobbie Campbell, after Rod, Fred and I had gone home, did avail himself of the opportunity of two weeks leave in Kenya. Unfortunately it turned out to be a six week stint - he caught malaria three days into the trip and was hospitalised - the nearest poor old Bobbie got to a Safari was walking the hospital grounds.

Another little trip I missed out on - and a trip I would have loved I know - was a ride around the great natural harbour that Aden boasts.

Fred Nurk, (a trained Wireless Operator of course) as I have said before, was transferred to the Air Sea Rescue section berthed on the Maala straight, which was situated about midway between Khormaksar and Steamer Point. His new place of work consisted of a small single story office alongside a purpose built jetty, which jutted out into the harbour, to which was moored a magnificent converted Motor Torpedo boat which was used solely for rescue should a plane have to ditch in the sea. Thankfully, in my time it was never called into action, but twice each week it went out on practice runs to make sure all was in working order. Fred had asked his superior if I could perhaps accompany them on such a trip, but he wouldn't allow it.

I was, however, allowed to visit the site when Fred was on one of his many lonely vigils, when he would make a brew and we would sit

OFF TO THE ASTRA

The lads meet at the Authors bed space
Left to right – Fred Nurk, Bobbie Campbell, Taff Waldroff, Fat Fred, Author
Note the 'Famous' mug on the locker

GET YOUR KNEES BROWN

It looks like pay day!

Back row left to right – Fred Nurk, Bobbie Campbell, Aubrey ?
Middle row left to right - ?, Rod Hamill, Taff Waldroff, Barrie Williams, ?, Author, ?
Front row left to right – Dave Shortman, Curley Goddard, Fat Fred

THE OLD BAZAAR IN CAIRO

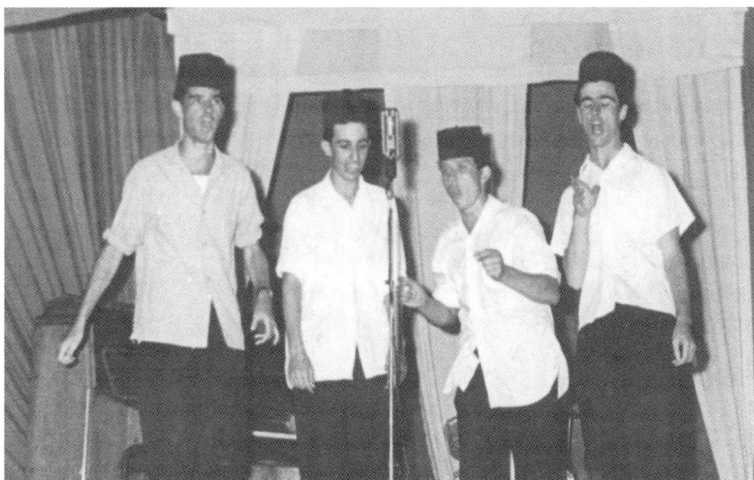

Rod Hamill, Fred Nurk, Bobbie Campbell and the Author
Airman's Club Variety Show

YOU CALLED ME BOSS?

THE ORIGINAL BOY BAND
ADEN 1957

Rod Hamill, Fred Nurk,
Bobbie Campbell and Author

No Recording contract
but what pretty boys?

The Author and Bobbie Campbell
miming to Stan Freeberg.
Show held at Khormaksar Airport

BLOCK FIVE MODELS

Fred Nurk, ? Rod Hamill and Bobbie Campbell

The lad standing between Fred and Rod was my next-door bedmate for
the entire fourteen months I spent in Aden and I have shamefully forgotten
his name. I haven't forgotten him though, or his marvellous book

FRED'S - FLUNKIES

Barry, Fred, John and The Author.
As Flunkies at the Corporals Club Khormaksar

THREE 'GIRLS' AND BORIS

Fred Nurk, Sue Pickles, Rod Hamill and the Author

Scene from Panto – 'Boris in the Woods'- performed for the families' wives and kids
One hot December afternoon in the Airman's Club

GIVE US A KISS

BORIS IN THE WOODS' – FINALE

Taff Waldroff, Sue Pickles, Joe Dent,
Bobbie Campbell, Fred Nurk,
The Author and Rod Hamill

Special evening performance
of the Panto for the boys

Boris (Rod Hamill) trying to
snatch a kiss from a very
reluctant Pricilla (The Author).

Not in the script I might add!

ALPINE BAR
Block Five - Bottom West

Fred Nurk and Joe Dent behind the bar
The Author far right next to Ian Rowe

ALPINE BAR
IN CONSTRUCTION

AIRMAN'S CLUB STAGE
ALMOST COMPLETE

The Author and Fred Nurk
Billet carpenters

The Author on stage
keeping a watching eye on proceedings

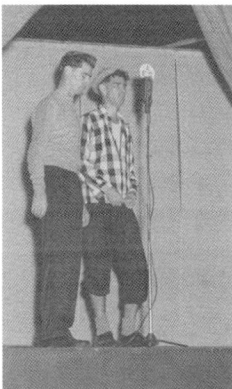

DOUBLE ACT

Rod Hamill (As Boris) and the Author
Airman's Club
In the midst of their popular double act

A HAPPY BUNCH OF ERKS

A gathering of lads taken in Block Five Middle West.
Back row left to right – The Author, Dave Shortman, ?, ?
Front – Bob Campbell, Phil Dodd, Barry Williams, Taff Waldroff, Fred Nurk, Aubrey

LOCAL ADEN BEAUTY

Dancing girl – Crater City
Note the narrow streets and ladder to the roof

CHUFF CHART

The Author standing by his locker pointing out that there are only days to go on his
'chuff chart' before he is blighty bound and demob.
Note 4d price tag 'borrowed' from a cheese sandwich at Paddington station.

ALL ABOARD

RAF bus – Ready to leave

RUNWAY REPAIRS

Bobbie Campbell on a bulldozer
repairing Khormaksar runway.
Note the Indian Ocean in the Background

ELEPHANT BAY

Note the shark nets to
Protect the swimmers!

FAREWELL TO ADEN

Back row left to right – Barry Williams, Fred Nurk, The Author, Bobbie Campbell,
Ian Rowe, ?, ?
Front row left to right – Curley Goddard, Taff Waldroff

The author, five minutes prior to boarding the Hastings (standing behind).
Leaving his mates, Aden, and the dreaded heat forever

ALRIGHT MY SON?

Monty welcomes home The Author

in the shade gazing across the blue/green water of the vast harbour, watching the Dhows plying their trade too and fro. Way across the water you could see the large oil holders at Little Aden and the enormous oil tankers that filled them. One of the most memorable occurrences during a visit was the sight of a vast shoal of - what looked like - baby Swordfish milling around the jetty. They weren't all that big, maybe a couple of feet long, but they had very long sword like noses and seemed aggressive little monkeys. I certainly would not have liked to have gone for a swim with them around. Mind you only a fool would try a swim in those waters at the best of times. Fred didn't fish but I must say, that little posting would have been paradise for a man that did.

Occasionally an old Arab crone would totter down the road begging. It was always the same one wrapped up in her rags, and she knew if she stayed at the wire fence long enough Fred would give her a bit of bread or a 10 cent piece. From memory a local could almost live for a day on 10 cents.

Looking back, although Aden provided me with a multitude of new experiences, for one reason or another I missed out on many more. Turtle watching on Bahrain Island, the palaces of Muscat and Oman, and perhaps most of all a Safari in Kenya and a chance to climb Kilamanjaro. What memories they would have provided - I could have written a book about them.

ADEN BLOWS HOT AND COOL

There were just two seasons in Aden.

The Hot season (120f plus) and the Cool season (90f plus).

Remarkably, there seemed to be no demarcation point between the two. One day it was the hot season, the next it was the cool. Both were very hot, but once you had experienced the hot season, the cool season was almost pleasant, with a daily temperature of around 90f. The problem was, no matter which time of the year, it never cooled own at night and the incessant humidity drained you constantly. Luckily the Signals block was air-conditioned and so for our working days it was most agreeable. Of course as soon as you walked out of the door you were greeted with a blast of hot air seemingly like a furnace. It was probably the reason for my Prickly Heat, which I suffered from for a lot of my stay. I must have been particularly allergic to it because few others seem to get it, and even nowadays when I go on holiday to hot climes, I can get a bout of it. I'm not moaning, for that heat definitely cured my Migraines, and I can tell you it was a marvellous swap for a bit of Prickly Heat.

Although I rarely checked a thermometer during my stay, the lowest temperature I ever saw was once whilst on guard duty. It was in the cool season, at 2am in the morning and the old mercury column read a mere 84f.

You could get used to the heat in time, but what really did you was the humidity. It was draining and relentless. It must have reached 90% or more at times. When I landed in Aden I was 12st 4lbs and within 10 weeks I had dropped to 9st. 12lbs. Mind you I had had my hair cut.

About six months into my tour an enterprising Indian gentleman opened a brand new cinema at Maala close to the Army barracks where our boys shared tents with The Aden Protectorate Levi.

The APL was a cross between the police and a local militia, and were made up of a few locals reinforced with a group of fit young men who were mainly Somali's. They did a reasonable job of keeping order and appeared to be well respected.

This Indian gentleman called his spanking new cinema - The Shanaaz. Unlike The Astra this luxurious picture house sported a roof and so required air conditioning. All very nice, until ten minutes before the interval, when the conditioning contrived to break down leaving the packed audience gasping for cold drinks and ice-cream. The enterprising Indian proprietor cashed in of course with bumper sales before miraculously 'fixing' the problem just in time for the start of the second half.

I only attended The Shanaaz once and that was to see that wonderful classic, "Gone With The Wind."

As with most of my cinema attendances I was immediately drawn into the film, and when the intermission came my emotions were running high, as indeed was my temperature.

Standing in the bar queue to get a cold coke, my heart leapt as there, standing with her back to me, was my girl from back home. Reaching forward to touch her shoulder, I was greeted firstly with a very angry Indian Gentleman, who I then realised was escorting her, and then to my horror, as she turned, the face (a very plain face) of the young lady who (from the rear) was the spitting image of my sweetheart.

Full of apology I made my way back to my seat - drink-less.

If that rather plain young lady had asked me at that moment in time, with the vision of a dozen very angry young Indians protecting her, if I minded being drink-less, I might have been tempted to say,

"Frankly my dear I don't give a damn."

Aden indeed could sometimes 'blow hot and cool.'

SPORT IN THE SUN

Sport took up a good deal of my time. We played football in the cool season, but I can assure you that was still quite draining. It suited me better than most as luckily I had reserves of stamina, and the heat slowed the speedsters down. Also, as control and passing, coupled with the ability to 'read' the game was my forte`, I could mostly let the ball do the work. I enjoyed my football, and played with and against some fine players. One of the lads I played against was a professional with Manchester United and immediately after the Munich air disaster he was allowed home and given a compassionate discharge I believe. On being demobbed I arrived at my home on the 30th April and dad had got me a ticket for the Man. United v Bolton Cup Final and I was surprised and delighted to see that the young lad from Aden was playing.

Although Signals had a fair team we didn't set the world alight, and I couldn't wait for the cricket to start.

My cricket in Aden was brilliant, and some of the highlights of the season are to be found in my book "66 n.o."- Tales of a Village Cricketer." Suffice to say, that I was sometimes playing two or three times per week, and although I opened the innings, and scored mountains of runs I never did managed to get a ton. I scored numerous 80's and 90's, but I kept getting out with the magic three figures close at hand. As you can imagine cricket was played in searing heat, and, as the sun went down at 6pm and it would be pitch dark at ten past six, we would start at one o'clock and have a couple of hours each in a forty over per side game. It was my first experience of this limited overs format, and I must say that I liked it, and was able to put that experience to good use later on in my cricket career, when playing for Stapleton.

The pitch was a strip of cocoanut matting and the outfield rolled hard sand. Although it was sand, it resembled shale as there was some grit in it and it wasn't too pleasant to go down on. It used to play havoc with the balls.

The boundary was at least 80 yards. Bats were tough old things (usually bound) and the balls were well worn on that unforgiving outfield. I remember one day mesmerising my teammates as I took one of the old balls from the battered old ammo box that housed them, and applying a bit of dear old Gordon Henderson's expertise and magic spittle, proceeded to turn the sad old relic into something almost new again. I bet that old Hambrook trick found its way around the country when the lads got back home.

It was in Aden that I was taught how to bowl at medium pace. My tutor was a lad called Tony Honeysett, who came from Essex I believe. He was a stocky individual and his bowling was as accurate as a Swiss watch. He rarely, if ever bowled a bad ball. He could get the odd delivery to swing away, which was something (try as I might) I could not do. In fact it was thirty years later before John Shepherd (West Indies - Kent - Gloucestershire) showed me how to do it. Too late in my career to be of any real use however, although I did baffled a few opponents whilst playing in the Stapleton seconds with my newly learned skill (and off only three paces at that).

With weather made for the beach and swimming and with the camp outdoor pool 200 yards only from the billet I enjoyed the water as did most of the lads, however, convenient as the camp pool was I much preferred swimming in the sea at Elephant Bay.

Although I tried Tennis I found it much too hot for this sport and stuck to cricket.

On a couple of occasions Fred dragged me off to watch the Camel racing on Khormaksar beach. It looked fun for the participants but as there was no betting allowed I could not enthuse for the sport. I did notice, however, that the Camels themselves definitely appeared to enjoy it and seemed very competitive. For certain the young Arab jockeys enjoyed spurring their mounts on and were ecstatic when they won.

As I have said, most sports were catered for on camp and Bobby Campbell enjoyed his Boxing and spent a good deal of his spare time training and sparring. In the unrelenting heat he never needed a sauna to make the weight, there wasn't an ounce of spare flesh on any of us.

I did attend the rifle range on a number of occasions in an attempt to win my Marksmans badge. The crack-shots on camp who regularly practiced on the range in the hope that they would be seconded into the biannual Pyard hunting party were my companions, and they encouraged me to succeed and join them, but I had no desire to shoot dogs, it was that illusive badge that I was after, and disappointingly I never did achieve that honour and I must have fired a thousand rounds and more with no success.

There's No Biz Like Show Biz

Another chunk of my time was taken up in the entertainment business. As told earlier, The Pentagons were formed and we wove our show around a series of mimes (mainly Stan Freeburg popular numbers of the day) This allowed Fred and Bobbie to get the 'feel' of the stage before blooding them further. Rod and I honed our double act with me playing the straight man and Rod using his incredible talent for humour, playing various characters that we created, the most popular being Boris, a seemingly half wit who invariably got the better of his (so called) superior (me).

Rod loved his musicals and his music, and was a great Bing Crosby fan. Although I enjoyed Bing, I preferred Frank Sinatra. This created a good-humoured point of discussion over the relative merits of the two crooners, and I had to put up with Rods never ending jossing. When the film " High Society" was shown, and Bing and Frank were in competition on the screen, he loved it. Particularly when Bing came out with the line, during one of their duets.

"You must be one of the newer fellows."

Rod, being a Welshman, of course had a good singing voice, and he despaired at the fact that none of his other three male partners could sing a note. It was a pity, but none of us could sing, and therefore it was something we were unable to use in our shows. However, Rod would often see a little something in a film musical that we could 'lift' and turn into a short 'dance' routine. These little 'dances' became very popular with our audiences, and we would be asked to perform them all over the place. Rod could dance, I should point out, but the rest of us had two left feet, which added to the fun. We had many hours of riotous fun rehearsing them, and when we did unveil them, the audience loved them too.

My sister Pam would send me each week, the latest jokes that she took from the radio, and so our act was always up to date.

When I wrote the Pantomime for Christmas 1957 we were able to get some other budding thespians to join us, which included a pretty little girl called Sue Pickles whose father was a Sergeant I believe. She was quite young and very nervous, but she sang like an angel and the lads loved her.

Though I say it myself, we really were quite good and (although Aden was starved of live entertainment) it was a pity that the powers that be did not encourage us more and let us take our shows around the Gulf.

One of our performances took place in the Aden Airport building at Khormaksar where the Miss Aden competition was being held. Now Rod being the joker he was, decided that we should all enter, (in drag of course), and sent in the application forms. It brought the house down. I remember wearing a swimsuit that Margaret had lent me and, as I thought, I looked quite fetching in it I was most disappointed when I finished last. We milked the audience for laughs and every one enjoyed the 'show,' although I do believe some of the genuine lady competitors were a bit disappointed that we upstaged them, and particularly when Fred Nurk got second prize wearing one of Margaret's mum's favourite dresses.

Mind you looking at the photos now, I can see how he fooled the judges.

We really did enjoy ourselves whilst entertaining the lads.

What with the bonus of having the very pretty, and greatly talented Margaret with us to remind us of home, and the pleasure of hearing the roars of approval from the very appreciative audiences, it made us all feel privileged to be part of the Show Biz world.

ADEN IN CONFLICT

For the entire duration of my stay in Aden, there was an undercurrent of discontent amongst the indigenous Arab population. Most of it was fuelled by Colonel Nasser in Egypt who, like many before him, had visions of grandeur, and had instigated the ill-fated Suez crisis by commandeering the canal and throwing us out. It is history now of course, but our attempt to retake control of the Suez flopped through lack of support from the Americans and most of the world too and we were made to eat humble pie and withdraw with our tail between our legs. Looking back on it forty odd years later, one can easily see that there is a great deal to be learned about diplomacy and alliances. Speaking as an Englishman, it is a great pity the world did not appoint our old diplomatic service to adjudicate over such matters. People generally speaking, would have been so much happier, and many more of them so much alive.

The only benefit to me at that time was, that it forced the RAF to fly me half way around Africa to get to Aden, and I saw a bit of the world (albeit but briefly) I would never otherwise have seen.

The day after Taff Nash and I went to Steamer Point to buy him a suitcase for his journey home, a bomb blew up the very café where we had sat and had enjoyed an ice-cold coke. That bomb blew three or four poor sailors to smithereens. I can understand perhaps some of the locals wanting us out, but there were 14000 troops stationed there, one way and another, and a large part of the populace were making a good living out of them.

As far as I could see we didn't interfere with their lives too much. On occasion I spent a few hours talking to an educated Arab, who worked on camp as a sort of liaison officer, about our presence there. He desperately tried to explain the Arabs dilemma. On balance he felt we should leave (which eventually we did) and let the area look after its own prosperity. Interestingly they must have been successful for down the years little is spoken of that, as was, crucial part of the world.

Apart from missing that bomb, and that large piece of masonry in Crater City, I personally only experienced one other dodgy situation, and at the time it was quite frightening.

Frightening it was, but once again my dad came to the rescue.

Three of us were winging our way back to camp in a taxi from a trip to Elephant Bay when, halfway up the Maala straight, the driver swung into one of the little camel market areas that lived under the overhanging mountain walls. It was obviously a pre-planned ploy as we were immediately surrounded by dozens of angry young Arabs. When I say angry, they were very angry, screaming and shouting and waving sticks and knives. A more villainous bunch of cutthroats you could not imagine. Most of them either carried or brandished those large curved Jambiya daggers so cherished by the tribesmen up-country. The lads now appreciated why old 'bracers and belt' Rog. always locked the door whenever I got into a taxi. As the mob screamed and yanked at the doors, for a split second I shit myself.

What to do? It was no good panicking.

Dear old dad and his wise old words saved me again.

'Never show fear son - look em in the eye - show authority.'

"Abdul - get this taxi out of here at once" I commanded.

"Do it - NOW."

The taxi driver, he now fearful thankfully, did as he was commanded, and in a cloud of dust we rejoined the road. Two miles further on, as we approached the Levi Police station, I reached over and switched off the engine and pocketed the ignition key. The car rolled to a stop right outside the front door. We quickly explained Abduls predicament to the duty Levi. He was led inside for questioning, and the Levi transported us the last couple of miles back to camp in their jeep.

As we walked through the camp gates to safety, and back to the billet, we all realised just how lucky we had been.

"What d'you think will happen to Abdul?" asked Fred.

"I don't know," I said, holding up his bunch of keys. "But unless he's got a spare set he will wish he hadn't trifled with us."

One thing that baffled me was the fact that all, and I mean all, the taxi drivers in Aden drove large modern Mercedes cars. There were literally hundreds of them about. Remember, this was 1957 and Aden was a British Protectorate. None of my mates, or for that matter anyone that I pointed it out to, seemed the slightest bit bothered about it, but even in those days I realised there was something dreadfully slack about our motorcar industry and it's salesmen. No wonder it went to the wall - sad isn't it?

THE DISAPPOINTING SIGNS

Here is another story about the Englishman abroad and it doesn't show him up in a very good light.

I was ordered, with a small group of fellow sportsmen, to help prepare the sports ground for the Command athletics tournament. We helped erect the large marques and the awnings to protect the seating from the sun. Around each area we erected a low white picket fence that separated the three marquee enclosures from each other, and when these were in place the Officer in charge of operations came up to me carrying three smart, newly painted signs.

"Put these in the appropriate enclosure laddie," he ordered.

I couldn't believe what he had handed me.

The signs read: -

'OFFICERS AND THEIR LADIES.'

'NCOs AND THEIR WIVES.'

'OTHER RANKS AND THEIR WOMEN.'

"With respect sir, I will let you erect those signs" I said, and put them on a chair and walked away.

Those obnoxious signs never saw the light of day, thank goodness, and the sports afternoon went with a swing.

THE DEVIL IN SKIRTS

I flew out to Aden with a dozen or so Black Watch soldiers, and it was they who were doing their duty tour of the Protectorate. They were tough, hard trained lads, and a fearsome opponent for anyone, never mind the cunning brave Yemeni tribesmen. They fought hard and drank hard, but although I did not get to know any of them personally, my admiration for them as soldiers knew no bounds. Details of their exploits up-country were fed through our signals office, and some of the situations these lads fought their way out of were mind-boggling. The tribesmen with their long 505 calibre rifles and curved daggers were a fearsome, cunning and, some say, brave foe. But apparently they were terrified of the Black Watch dressed in their kilts, bagpipes to the fore, marching toward their mountainous hideaways, and would invariably disappear without firing a shot.

'Devil women in skirts' they called them.

I have two strong personal memories of those lads.

One night a dozen or so had infiltrated our NAAFI and decided to build a pyramid with empty beer cans. The centre of the room was cleared of tables and the base of their pyramid was swiftly laid. Initially the edifice grew swiftly but as the evening progressed and the alcohol did its work, the construction began to slow down. Some of our lads weighed in with a can or two but the Scotsmen were determined to finish their work come what may. Eventually they completed their task, but how they managed to place that final can on the very top without bringing the whole work of art crashing down I will never know, but they accomplished it. Then followed a most extraordinary half hour of dancing to the swirl of the bagpipes, as round and round their edifice they leapt and pirouetted. I don't know whether anyone took any photos of that unique pyramid, but I hope they did, for it was no longer there the next morning.

On another occasion, a group of the Black Watch had been invited to the Families Club where The Pentagons were putting on a show. They all turned up looking very smart in their kilts and sporrans, and their wee Dirk (dagger) tucked in their stocking.

We did our bit on stage and then the Scots requested permission to do theirs. Placing a pair of crossed Claymores (swords) in the centre of the Terazelled dance floor that lay in the middle of the area, and with a piper playing a brisk tune on his bagpipes, these tough, hard bitten warriors, proceeded to dance in their stocking feet, as light as a feather, around those swords, skipping in and out of the wickedly sharp blades, floating like gossamer on the wind.

I, like everyone else there, was awestruck. I will never forget it.

The contradiction of strength and aggression with the gentleness and beauty of that dance was quite amazing.

When all those brawny lads had taken their turn to show the lightness of their feet, I turned to my fellow Pentagons and they, like me, were all shedding a tear.

They were tough lads those Scottish boys, hard as Aberdeen granite, but I was fortunate enough to see the gentler side of those proud fighting men and I was privileged to know them.

SAND IN MY EYES

One day as a sandstorm was gradually clearing (the effect of same, for those of you that have never experienced one, is visually, not unlike a pea souper fog.) I came, once again, within an ace of leaving this world. We were standing on the balcony of Block 5 Middle West with our towels wrapped around our faces, when we heard the roar of aero engines screaming at full throttle and a Beverly briefly appeared through the dust, flying straight at us, headlights blazing, before it disappeared, vanishing into the gloom as it skimmed the roof of the block.

It was literally feet above us. The poor pilot, we surmised, had come in to land mistaking the Maala Straight street lights for the landing strip.

The problem with that theory was that the Maala Straight was at right angles to the Khormaksar runway and our billet blocks were in the way. He must have got down OK because we never heard a big bang.

Whatever the reason, if he hadn't pulled that joystick when he did I would not be writing this now.

A RARE DELIGHT

One of the occasional delights we enjoyed, was the appearance outside of the camp perimeter on the Sheik Othman road of (would you believe it) a fish and chip van. It was run by a very amiable Arab and his hard working boy.

Now, this fellow had been warned off many times by the Military Police, but had somehow, (by some secret code no doubt), managed to turn up, out of the blue, about once a month to ply his trade. When he did arrive, word spread like wild fire, and literally hundreds of airmen would make the long trek (it was always on the darkest of nights that he came) to the hole that had been conveniently cut in the perimeter fence, and avail themselves of Abdul's delicious fare. Although we were surrounded by the sea, fish never ever appeared on our menu, and so when Abdul arrived he was a very popular man. It was home from home as you walked back across the sand with your chips (real potatoes) and a large piece of unknown but delicious fish, in your self-supplied container (no newspapers available out there) liberally covered in salt and vinegar. Thinking about it now, that Arab must have been a genius because he always had piping hot fish and chips ready to serve, and there was never a queue of more than a dozen or so. How did he do it?

Food mark you, was always on everyone's mind, as try as they might the poor old cooks were fighting a constant battle to feed us properly. There were virtually no fresh vegetables (I only once had a proper potato served in the mess, and that was for my Christmas dinner). Everything came out of a tin and most of it was powdered, from eggs to potato. The meat (mostly) was fresh but even that, as it lay sliced on the serving tray, would be tinged green on the edges that were exposed to the air. I ate it. I can't tell you what it was I was eating, or what it tasted like. It was probably Camel or Goat. The cooks tried to please us with our puddings, and gave us treacle tart or ginger sponge to try to augment the weak Tapioca or gooey Rice pud. The custard (when you got it) was insipid stuff that tasted vile, but it was never refused as it was used to soften the usually rock hard sponge that had dried out in the heat. I came to look forward to my baked beans on fried bread, which I now enjoyed, (thank you

Blackbush Airport). They were not beans as we know them, but a gooey clot of pink morass slopped onto a large slice of fried bread. The fried bread was fried rock hard in camel fat, or some such concoction, but the combination of the two and its cloying consistency I began to get used to, and then eventually enjoy. I sometimes yearn for a plate of those beans and its accompanying fried bread to this day.

One thing for sure, it really was a unique flavour.

On Christmas day the cooks made a special effort. We had Turkey and fresh potatoes with all the trimmings and a proper Christmas pud. The Officers turned out in force, and acting as waiters served us at the table. They were really good sports, handling all the obvious banter in good humour. We even had sparkling white tablecloths and the odd festive bauble scattered along the tables. We sang carols and had much fun as we ate our tinned turkey, before returning to our billets to lay quietly thinking of home. For a while the old billet was a sombre place before someone broke the mood and opened a bottle. I for one missed not being at home, and luckily in the whole of my life that is the only time that I have been away at Christmas.

As I say, the cooks made a special effort for our Christmas dinner and the tables were all covered with tablecloths. The only other time that I saw those tablecloths was when Duncan Sandys, the defence Minister of the time, paid us a visit. We were all sat at the table when he arrived at the mess followed by the C.O. and all of his entourage.

There was more 'scrambled egg' (officers in full dress uniform) on display than at a boy scouts jamboree breakfast.

As the Minister and his crocodile of officers slowly walked around the long tables, he would stop occasionally and speak to the men. He stopped right opposite me, smiled and said,

"Everything alright gentlemen?"

"It is today sir," said Barry Williams, the lad sat right under his person. "But if you had come yesterday or you come tomorrow, you will see things differently."

Slightly shaken the Minister's face hardened.

"You have nothing to complain about Airman as far as I can see" he growled, and walked on.

We all took a deep breath as first the Group Captain, and then one by one his entourage, glowered at Barry before the duty officer reached our position and said icily, "Take down this Airman's complaint Sergeant."

Nothing was said or done about it of course. Our food was still as poor as ever.

Ours wasn't too good, but what about those poor old bloody Black Watch up-country.

CHRISTMAS FAR FROM HOME

To try and keep the lads minds occupied from thinking too much about home at Christmas time, the powers that be encouraged each billet to build a bar and take part in a camp competition to find the best creation. The prize for the winning billet was copious amounts of alcohol to stock it.

Our beds were moved up the billet leaving a space at the bottom of the room where a bar was constructed. Each billet used a theme for their efforts and many far-fetched and exotic ideas were put together in the weeks leading up to the big day. Our lads went for sophistication and decided to build 'The Alpine Bar.' Although I helped a little, I must confess I spent more time watching the carpenters amongst us having fun than actually building anything. Although their efforts were (in my view) excellent, we didn't get even an honourable mention. To the delight of Rod and Bobbie their 'Moulin Rouge' effort in Block 5 Middle West (the floor directly above us) stole the prize money. Take it from me ours was better, and I have photographs of both to prove it.

Most of the lads were pretty stoical about being away from their loved ones, but as I said before, I found it pretty hard. This was the second Christmas that poor old Rod and Bobbie had been away from home, as of course had many of the other lads, and so they at least knew what to expect.

Most of our Christmas mail arrived a week late, which didn't help matters, and of course there was no way that you could phone home.

My recollections of that particular Christmas festival was that of a pretty grim occasion, with not much for me to celebrate.

Yes, I will always remember Christmas 1957

LIFE'S LITTLE PLEASURES

Apart from sunstroke, provided you drank plenty and kept your salt levels up you had a good chance of staying fit. As explained earlier, plenty of salt tablets were available on the tables in the mess and there were Lemon and Orange crystals too. The crystals were there to encourage you to drink more water, which was desalinated and was lukewarm to boot, and tasted dreadful when neat. The problem was that if you made your crystal drink too strong you could end up 'peeing razor blades.' For me I stuck largely to Issam's chai, and my mug was rarely empty.

One of my little pleasures in life was a daily mug of chai (foul that it was and tasted nothing like tea), and a small pack of five Huntley and Palmer custard cream biscuits, which I dunked in the warm liquid. That tea was made with goat's milk and desalinated water, but well sweetened one became used to it and its unique taste. My head swims even now as I remember the pleasure of those five little beauties, and I savoured each and every one. I have forgotten what Issam used to charge me for my custard creams but it was about 5 East African cents (about 6d - 2.5p).

Because of the heat and high humidity, frequent showers were a must, and if you didn't keep a constant watch over your crotch and under your arms then you could end up with Tinea (ringworm). Tinea was easily treated by the medic who would issue you with a little jar of cream to rub on it, but if not dealt with swiftly, it could spread all over your body in no time. It was highly infectious, but the lads were very good at containing it. Luckily I only got it once and that was the tiniest dot, which was gone in a couple of days. I remember one bloke in our billet, who came from Leicester, who decided that he was going to keep his Tinea a secret. When eventually one of the lads caught sight of him in the showers covered in the dreaded lurgi, he was thrown out of the billet, and driven off to sick bay. His outbreak was so bad he was actually hospitalised. What a fool, and all for a small jar of cream.

You kept out of the sun of course, but even then you went, in no time at all, brown as a nut. It was here that I learnt to 'shade bathe.' In later years when I used to go to Tenerife with my mates, whilst they would lie out in the sun for hours on end, slapping on tubes and tubes of sun cream, I would sit in the shade reading a book. To their annoyance I was just as brown as they were on the plane going home.

Try it - 'shade bathing' - it really works, and it's healthier.

The currency in Aden was East African Cents and the cost of living was extremely low. Twenty Capstan Full Strength cigarettes were about 1/- and a bottle of Coke about 6d. A taxi ride from Steamer Point to camp (less than 10 miles) cost about 3/- and a ride on a bus for the same journey about 3d.

I only ever had one meal away from camp, (other than those delicious fish and chips) and that was in an Arab restaurant in Crater City where we had a Goat steak and chips and a pint of Coke for about 2/6.

The Arabs, although they used East African currency on a daily basis, still traded in the ancient Maria Theresa Thaler (dollar). These handsome silver coins came originally from the Austro-Hungarian Empire of 250 years ago and were greatly treasured by the Yemenis. I do regret not bringing one home as a memento.

They were quite large coins and heavy. Made of solid silver with the head of (I believe) Empress Maria Theresa on one side and the Hapsburg Double Eagle on the back. I do know that up until 1958 they were still minted, and remarkably they all bore the same date (1780). I have vivid memories of walking up the very narrow 'Money changers' street in Crater where many ancient looking Arabs sat crossed legged in their shop doorway with piles of the said silver dollars in front of them, and riffling them from one hand to the other as they touted for trade. The metallic shhhhhink - shhhhink as the coins returned to hand was another unique noise I shall never forget.

As a matter of interest Empress Maria Theresa ruled for 40 years between 1740 and 1780 and had no less than 16 children - one of which was the ill fated, and guillotined, Marie Antoinette.

In fourteen months in Aden I made many, many, marvellous friends but my close buddies were Rod Hamill, who came from Llanelli and was a proud Welshman, Bobbie (jock) Campbell who came from Glasgow and was an equally proud Scotsman, and Bernard (Fred Nurk) O'Donaghue who came from London. We did most things together, although sport sort of divided us.

Bobbie was a boxer and a very good one too.

He won the Command middleweight title, and his training took up a large chunk of his free time. Fred, apart from his Snooker, was an avid spectator and seemed to enjoy playing his football and cricket through my exploits, whilst Rod thought we were all fools chasing about in the heat, and although he enjoyed a swim, chose more relaxing pastimes.

There were many other smashing blokes sharing the sun with me and sadly, I am ashamed to say, I have forgotten most of their names. There was a couple of lads that joined Fred and I when we were asked to act as waiters in the Corporals club for one of their regular 'fun' nights. We did this job on a number of occasions and not only were we well paid for our efforts, but Fred taught us how to extract extra tips from the partying NCOs and their families. His little 'tricks' are probably still used to this day.

For example: make sure all the client's change is in small coin. They don't want a pocket full of copper and so wave you off with it.

Leave the change (if it is made up of silver etc.) in a puddle of beer on the tray (who wants a pocket full of wet change?). Accept their offer of 'one for yourself' and add on the price of a small beer to the bill but pocket the money etc etc.

His best bit of advice however was, 'never ever short change the punter, for if you do, invariably he will notice and the word will get around and your tips will disappear.'

Fred was a little genius and most charming in his manner (which helped secure even larger tips). He always did much better than we did, and always generously shared his extra booty with us.

"It's your job Rog. so you might as well make it pay" he used to say.

Later on in life when I was teaching young girls how to man my lottery kiosks whist working for Gloucestershire County Cricket Club, and also selling the lottery tickets at the cricket matches, I passed on those lessons, learned in the desert, on how to get the punter to spend a few coppers more.

Dear old Fred and his waiter's tricks helped immensely, in my quest to swell the County Cricket Club's coffers.

It's On The Cards

One of the pastimes the four of us shared was a game of cribbage. We played regularly and we always used Rod's bed as our card table. Rod and Bobbie lived in Block 5 Middle West, and so it became a regular billet challenge with Fred and I representing Block 5 Bottom West against the men above. These games were always keenly fought and we took pride in winning. Our crib sessions ended, however, when one day with Fred and I needing about forty holes to win and Rod and Jock only two, Rod said,

"Game over boys - pay up."

We used to play for 5 cents a game, but it wasn't the money that mattered it was the winning that counted, and all games were fought out with dogged determination. Me being me, insisted that we hadn't yet lost.

Rod, in good humour, said,

"Your not going to make us deal out another hand are you? You've got no chance."

"But you haven't won yet" I said.

After much heated argument I had my way and the cards were shuffled and dealt.

Rod and Jock pegged but one only, whilst we pegged five or six.

It was Fred's take and remarkably he had twenty-four. Jock, in despair, revealed a 'nineteen hand' whilst I held fourteen to pip them on the post.

It was the most unlikely win ever.

Rod, who was the most amiable of men normally, tossed the cards in the air and said that he didn't want to play anymore.

Rather than break up a wonderful friendship, neither we did.

Prepare For Home

About a month before my demob I was summoned to see a senior Officer in the Education Block. Sitting me down, he smiled and remarked that it looked as though I had had a super time in the RAF and of course I would be signing on. Shocked, I hurriedly told him that he must have the wrong man as I was looking forward to going home and demob. He asked me to give him one good reason why I shouldn't become a professional Airman, and appeared surprised when I told him that the one thing I was looking forward to as a civilian was, after coming home from a good days work, being able to sit down to my evening meal knowing that the door would not open and someone would order me to get dressed and go up onto the road and guard a hole.

And that I would have no choice - I would have to do it.

He blinked hard on hearing this, made a note on my records and simply said "I wish you well in your civilian life" and shook my hand.

Eventually the time for me to go home arrived.

It was a very exciting time, and although you knew you were leaving behind all your pals and a way of life you would never experience again, the sadness of that was tempered by the fact that you knew that they too would all be 'on the boat' pretty soon too. I was pretty lucky really as I was second of our little group of pals to go home, (Rod having found a seat on a Beverley just two weeks before) and this time I was not going to be 'left alone' as had happened to me a couple of times before in my RAF life.

So it seemed that those fourteen 'back flighted' days, and the time I had spent in pool flight at Hednesford with Howard and his 'goldmine', had shortened my Aden tour.

In retrospect, a fair swap.

I must confess I did feel sorry for some of the lads, particularly Bobbie, who had been there when I arrived, and then saw me leaving him behind. Poor old Bobbie still had five months to do, and most of that would be during the hot season.

Most of the lads made a big thing of going home. They would organise a 'boat party' and celebrate their coming big day by getting paralytic drunk. But this was not my way.

I did hold a party, but mine was two or three days before my departure, and I did not want to overdo the drink.

Many of my mates thought I was a spoilsport, but firstly I wasn't too keen on drinking, and secondly I wasn't going to risk getting ill (like some had done) and miss my plane. I had seen lads so drunk that they were carried back to their billet, stripped off, and flung in the showers with a large bow of ribbon tied around their John Thomas with a notice alongside stating,

'I'M COMING HOME - HERE'S A PRESENT FOR YOU.'

There would then be many photographs taken of the inebriated airman, as witness to a successful 'boat party.'

With my deep-sea trunk packed and away six weeks before, I awaited my call with suitcase and kit bag ready. You would think that I would remember the date that I took off from Khormaksar in that converted Hastings, but I cannot be sure.

It was, I guess, about 27th April 1958.

I honestly can't remember a thing about that final day. I don't remember leaving the billet and my comforting little bed space, or saying goodbye to any of my billet mates. Or even how I got to the airport. Luckily for me, and my lapsed memory, a couple of photographs were taken at the airport to remind me of that day. When I look at them now, I still find that I have no recollection whatever of those life changing moments. Yet I can remember winging skywards and past old Shamsan for the last time. It must have been the excitement of knowing that I was at last going home and getting to see all my loved ones again after such a long time.

I certainly had missed home.

In the fourteen months that I was there I had experienced dreadful homesickness only three or four times, unlike some of the lads who had suffered badly. Homesickness is an awful thing. You are overcome with a feeling of great desperation and an overwhelming feeling to run away.

But there was nowhere to run.

You simply had to grit your teeth, perhaps shed a tear or two, and get on with it.

At least we knew the date that we were to go home. Goodness knows what those brave soldiers must have gone through during the war when they had no idea when (or if) they would ever see home again.

Fortunately my homesickness bouts lasted but fleetingly, and when they did come along my mates cheered me up, as I did with them when their turn came.

At least I did not have to endure a 'Dear John...' like a lot of the lads.

Now that took a lot of getting over, and many tears were quietly shed and compensatory alcohol consumed. If only those unfeeling girls could have known the anguish they brought to their boys far from home, as they penned those insensitive words.

It was a tough life sometimes being a National Serviceman.

But my Chuff Chart was full up, and I had been given my departure date, and although there was a little sadness in leaving my mates and the desert behind, my thoughts were now on home and my loved ones.

Goodbye Aden forever.

Gone but never to be forgotten.

Goodbye Sunshine

The lads came to the airport and gave me a rousing send off. Luckily for me there are two or three super photographs taken recording that moment, for as I have said, I cannot remember a thing about it. I was second to leave of our little group and I did feel for them. But their turn was to come. I was on the plane (another converted RAF Hastings) and winging my way home, but this time in pretty much a straight line, as the Suez conflab was now history.

I bade Shamsan goodbye for the last time from my aircraft window as we passed close by, and up into the ever clear blue desert sky of Aden.

We flew up the Yemeni coast for a while before we crossed the Red Sea and headed inland.

Some hours later we landed at Wadi Halfa near Khartoum in the Sudan to refuel. Wadi Halfa was on the river Nile, and although I only saw the river from the air, I certainly got the full impression of how those mighty waters could change the history of the world. We were allowed to get off the plane for an hour or so to stretch our legs, and I particularly remember the blast of very hot air that hit my face as I got to the aircraft door. It was a different heat to Aden. This was a dry heat, and I must say did seem to be even hotter than where I had just come from, and every bit as uncomfortable. At least I got to briefly experience the heat that General Gordon had felt in more senses than one, when the poor man found himself and his brave soldiers in a very hot spot all those years ago.

Next stop was Benghazi; an historic name in the annals of war if ever there was one. We had four or five hours there, and although it was slightly cooler than Khartoum, it was still pretty hot.

I was amazed to see alongside the airfield the enormous military weaponry graveyard that was still there some thirteen years after the war had ended. There were tanks and lorries and large field guns all heaped up in this grotesque pile, and all rusting away.

A monument to man's stupidity and his lust for conquest.

'Thirteen years have gone by and they still haven't learnt a thing' I thought.

On across the Mediterranean we flew towards Marseilles.

It was during this hop that I decided to ask if I could visit the front of the plane. I explained to the Squadron Leader and his fellow crew members, that having served two years in the RAF and not having seen the inside of a cockpit, it would be nice to at least see what my efforts had been all about.

The crew were most friendly and obliging, and explained how everything worked. The flight engineer showed me how he 'tuned' each of the four engines to get the maximum efficiency out of them. He explained and showed me (by making slight adjustments to each engine) how, when all the engines were in sync. there was virtually no vibration. The Navigator explained his duties and he too showed me how he was able to ascertain our position. He lost me completely in his well-meaning explanation, and I was glad they were not relying on me to guide us home. When the Captain invited me to sit in his co-pilot's seat and play at being Biggles I jumped at the chance. I was taken back 10 years to when, as a little boy a kindly officer, just like this one, had allowed me to sit in his Meteor that was parked alongside the runway at Filton and fight the Battle of Britain all over again. This equally kindly Officer let me 'feel' the rudder with my feet and at the same time, taking the joy stick in my hands, he let me fly the plane (he said) for five minutes or so. I must say, I do remember feeling that this giant bird was (albeit only momentarily) under my control.

As we approached Marseilles (it was getting dark and I could see the lights of the port shining up ahead) I was sent back to my seat, but not before I had heard Marseilles control tower call us up and indicate that we were clear to land, and that they were awaiting us.

At Marseilles we were given some food in their welcoming restaurant and it felt good to be back on European soil.

Back in the air for the last leg of my journey home and I was really getting excited.

It was dawn and the sun was shining as we crossed the Channel.

All at once there below us, bathed in spring sunshine, was England.

How green she looked. I'd almost forgotten what green fields looked like. My spirits rose.

Off loaded and straight on to a train, and across those green fields to Gloucester. This time that train journey was over in a flash.

Off the train and onto a waiting RAF wooden slated seat bus (shades of Entebbe and those lush banana plantations) that whisked us through the crowded town, and then through the welcoming gates of RAF Innsworth - Gloucester.

Back to where I had started my adventure some fourteen months before.

I was now just 30 miles from home. - Almost there.

We were welcomed, debriefed, fed and given some good old English money. I was given a train ticket to Bristol Temple Meads, and wished all good fortune in my future life.

Onto the RAF bus once more and a short ride to the station at Gloucester. But this time I boarded the train as a civilian.

It felt good.

It was April 30th 1958.

I had done my duty, and I was going home.

THE FINAL STEPS HOME

The train was packed and I had to stand, but this time I didn't mind.

I was nearly home.

It was then, as I stood there in the corridor, that I realised that everyone around me were sunburnt. I had thought, as I travelled home, that my nut brown tan would be eye catching, and I would at least have one thing to show for my fourteen months away.

But there I was, standing amongst equally brown and healthy looking travellers. What I hadn't known was that England had just experienced an unprecedented two-week April heat wave.

Did it matter? Not a bit. I was home at last.

Getting off the bus at Pye Corner, and with my kit bag over my shoulder, and my suitcase in my hand, I walked down the lane and to home. As I rounded the final bend I was greeted with squeals of delight by my baby sister Wendy who I barely recognised as she was fast growing up. Dropping my bags in the lane I enjoyed the hugs and kisses of home that I had so much missed.

Indoors mother was waiting, with fourteen months of love and cuddles, all saved up for me and this moment.

"Your father's in the garden" mother said eventually, wiping away a tear.

How like dad: let the women folk have their time first.

There he stood, garden fork in his hand, wearing his favourite cap and his Fair Isle pullover, and puffing on his well used pipe.

"Alright my son" he said.

That's all - nothing more, just as if I had only been away for a day. But I could see he was pleased and proud.

Mother called us both in for a welcome 'proper' cup of tea.

No more chai made with desalinated water - a proper cup of tea.

"I've got a nice bit of pork for your tea" said mother, "And your father has managed to get some Jersey Royals to go with it."

Real potatoes - and Jersey Royals at that. - Well done dad.

Enough said - I was home alright, and I was a very happy young ex-airman.

Mother produced some of her freshly baked cakes to go with my cuppa but was not hurt when I said,

"I wouldn't mind a piece of cheese mum."

In an instant father had produced the largest piece of cheddar cheese, still sporting its rind, you ever did see. I took it from its plate and sank my teeth into it.

It was delicious.

Savouring that cheese, I explained that the only cheese we ever saw in Aden was that rubbery tasteless stuff, and there was not too much of that. I told them that I had had numerous nightmares dreaming about cheese, and couldn't wait for the day I would taste a piece of decent Cheddar once more. My nightmares invariably found me (for some reason) trapped in a dark cellar for hours on end before, eventually, high above me, a trap door opened. My relief at seeing light however, was short lived, as hundreds of big round cheeses were thrown in on top of me. Down they would fall, crushing me, and all the while I was unable to eat even a mouthful.

I learned by experience exactly how Ben Gunn must have felt alone on his Treasure Island, and longing for 'a piece of cheese for a Christian man.'

As I told my story with my little sister skipping around me excitedly, I suddenly realised that I had scoffed the lot.

"Sorry dad" I said, "I didn't realise that I had missed it that much."

"Plenty more where that came from son" he said, "Good to have you home. Now don't go putting your name down for cricket next Saturday - because I've got you a ticket for the Cup Final at Wembley."

My homecoming was almost complete.

I enjoyed my lovely roast pork meal, with real potatoes, and I fancy mothers cooking was even better than ever before.

I then set out for Manor Park Hospital, and a surprise for my pretty young Persian Princess.

Parvin

My Persian Princess

INDEX